All Scriptures take from the KJV unless otherwise indicated.

Freshwater Press

USA

First Printing 2003,

Second Printing 2022

MARRIAGE ED., Rules of Engagement & Marriage

ISBN: 978-1-960150-40-0

MARRIAGE ED.

Rules of Engagement & Marriage

Freshwater

Freshwater Press

USA

Dedication

MARRIAGE ED. is dedicated to everyone who is:

- Wise enough to seek God before marriage,
- Brave enough to get married.
- Courageous enough to stay married,
- Wise enough to seek God throughout their marriage,
- Obedient enough to the Lord, to be victorious in marriage.

MARRIAGE ED. is dedicated to the dedicated--, those who take God, life, and marriage seriously.

Foreword

If the purpose of being saved is Marriage to the Lamb, why don't Christians (especially) take marriage more seriously?

Are you saved? Yes? Good.

When you're ready to take your salvation

up a notch--, get married.

The Bible says to work out your salvation with fear and trembling (Phil 2:12b); you should get married with the same respect of the Marriage Covenant; work your marriage with respect and sobriety.

Could you imagine, after what you consider a successful Christian life, getting to the Pearly Gates and having your application for entrance stamped:

NOT MARRIAGE MATERIAL

just because you refused to get married or wouldn't stay married because it was *too much work*?

Oh my!

4

Table of Contents

Preface

The Lord had me praying in the Book of Ephesians for an extended season. Ephesians, Chapter 5 is commonly quoted for marriages, but Holy Spirit instructed me that ALL of the Book of Ephesians can be applied to marriage, so that is what I am sharing in this little book. Each "Rule" of marriage is taken from the Ten Commandments, or nearly line upon line from the Book of Ephesians to teach, comfort, exhort, and even admonish you as you are given Wisdom, knowledge and understanding to know if you're ready for marriage, or how to be more efficient at marriage if you are already wed. The "Rules" are supported by other Scriptures, because in the counsel of two or three shall every Word be established.

You will find transforming power in the Word of God. MARRIAGE ED., *Rules of Engagement and Marriage*, is packed with the Word of God, and has the power to transform you, your mate, and your marriage into what the Word says a marriage should be.

Just as you have a Driver's Education Manual that you must study and learn before taking the Driver's licensing test, here is the MARRIAGE ED. MANUAL *Rules for Engagement and Marriage.* Study this book before getting your marriage license. If already married, this book will refresh you, or teach you things that you should have already learned. Married or planning to get married--, you need **MARRIAGE ED.**

Introduction

Marriage is more than an arrangement; it is a spiritual covenant. You must meet certain spiritual requirements and be *spiritual* to be successful in marriage. You cannot only be *spiritual*, standing before the preacher on your wedding day, you must remain spiritual, in the Spirit, and in the *spirit of your marriage* to have a successful marriage, as two *become* one. Two becoming one is a spiritual process, accomplished by the Spirit when two are *at least* cooperating with the Spirit, and remaining (as much as it is possible) *in* the Spirit.

Marriage is not an event, it is a *process*, a discipline, and a lifestyle. The wedding is the event, not the marriage.

All Disciplines have fruit; marriage has fruit, and we will discuss some of it in this manual, and also, the Fruit of Marriage, what I call *The Promise*.

When you marry someone, what you are saying to God is that you desire and expect to become connected to your mate, *spiritually*. That is a huge statement. Yes, the Bible says that two *become* **one flesh,** but it also says that man's body (flesh) is the temple of the Holy Spirit. Before marriage, the condition of his or her temple must be considered, because you will join to whatever *spirit* or *spirits* that are in your potential mate when you marry. As a result of marriage, two become joined *spiritually*. So, Pre-marrieds', you should endeavor to know EVERY *spirit*, every spiritual influence; as well, the spiritual history of not only your intended spouse, but also the generational influences of your intended mate's family, and family history, *before* marriage.

Still, all the ways of a man are clean in his own eyes (Proverbs 16:2). This means you should also know EVERY *spirit*, every spiritual influence, the spiritual history of not only **yourself**, but of **your entire family** as well--, back at least four generations. Knowing all of this information doesn't indicate what's in your *temple*, it only says what has been or *could be* in there.

I want my spirit to be joined to his or her spirit, is what you say to God when you get married. That's deep. You can't pick and choose--, it's the whole enchilada. *"Some things I like about him or her, some things I don't like."* Some things I will have to change about him or her, et cetera." When you marry, you get your **whole** spouse, not just the parts you *like*.

Entering into relationship with Jesus, <u>we</u> must be changed, we become transformed, renewed. We have to change because we are dead in sin and trespasses until Jesus invites us into relationship with Himself. That is a vertical invitation. He is inviting us up from the depths of sin, despair, and even spiritual death…, up—into life and eternal life. This is not only a promotion, but also **Resurrection**!

When you marry another human being, that is a lateral, not a vertical move; you do not have life, and that more abundantly to offer another person. Only Jesus Christ has that. You cannot change him or her to be what you want them to be to be with you. You just don't have it like that. No man, or woman has any obligation to another man or woman to *change* to be in relationship, except by and because of Jesus Christ.

Rule 1: No Change

No Change! (We are not talking about coins left over from the grocery money!) **Don't expect to change anything--, not one thing about your mate from the first day you meet him or her.** Dating is to learn, discover, and enjoy what's already there, not to *change* it. You may be one to get up in the morning to watch the sunrise--, you enjoy it, you don't comment to yourself or God what needs to be done to make it better. Just as with the sunrise, as the light of discovery illuminates your mate--, as the sunlight of your eyes rises on him or her, (who is also God's creation), revealing things that you may not have before seen--, enjoy him or her, don't criticize or critique God's work. Anything about your mate or intended mate that you absolutely can't stand, you'd better learn how to *stand*. Pray that your mate will allow **God** to change him or her or learn to accept him or her as is. If there are many things you don't enjoy or can't tolerate—if you have not yet married, perhaps this is not the one, or not the season to wed.

The Serenity Prayer: *Lord, give me the Serenity to accept the things that I cannot change, Courage to change the things I can, and Wisdom to know the difference.*

After diapers, it's difficult to change anyone. Even if your mate or intended mate is acting as though they should be in *Pull Ups*, you can't change anything about him or her. Accept it. Put up with it. Wait on God, after you pray.

If you're praying to God to change your mate and he or she is not doing so fast enough, you'd better pray more. Pray more fervently, and for the ability to be forbearing, longsuffering, patient and accepting.

Who do you know who has ever said, *"I can't wait to get married so my husband or wife can change me"*? No one. You cannot change anyone. No one is expecting change at your hands; so, don't offer. Manage your expectations.

But Jesus expects us to change. Yup, and He will get what He wants out of us. We aren't yet married to Jesus. Marriage to the Lamb is a prophetic promise, and we are in the daily process of trimming our lamps (Matt 25-1:7), transforming, renewing (Rom 12:2) and *becoming*, to get into a proper earthly and glorious eternal relationship with Him. If you're alive, you will change. Have you ever seen a tree whose leaves refused to change with the season? It was dead, wasn't it? But change is only at the Hand of God, by the Spirit of the Lord, and by the will of the one being changed--, not by another man or woman.

You may already be married. If your mate is getting on your nerves, you should have waited for him or her to *become* fully transformed, first. But, since you didn't wait, if he or she had been waiting on you to change, if everyone waited, **no one** would be married today. This is why we all need both Faith and Grace. We all need to give Grace because no one is perfect; Jesus is the only Perfect Man.

So, there you are, an imperfect being marrying, or married to an imperfect being. Expect that instead of perfection, and deal with it. Enjoy it. You're human, find out how to appreciate the perfect things about your imperfect mate and how to help, and/or be patient about the imperfect things. That's what he or she has to do for you.

All the while you are living and especially if married, you are in the *process* of maturing and reaching toward perfection. But while married you are in a constant state of flux. Life is dynamic. If things aren't constantly changing in and around you, something is dead. Thank God for life!

So, you begin the process of marriage, which is really the process of *becoming* a marriage partner.

You're not a marriage partner when you're dating; you're a marriage *candidate*. You are not a marriage partner when you are walking down the aisle or standing at the altar; the ceremony is merely an event. The dress and the tuxedo make you a bride or a groom, but not a wife or a husband; they are only clothes. You're a candidate; *give the candidate a hand!*

After the ceremony, begins the process of *becoming*. You must **become**. Your mate must *become*. Both of you must *become together*--, **all at the same time**. Those transformations, **all at the same time** is one of the main reasons that marriage is not easy. That's why the husband needs the *Husband's anointing* and wife needs the *Wife's anointing*; those anointings are only given from God as a wedding gift to two who are married.

As we prepare for marriage to the Lamb, He is allowing us time on Earth, to *become*. Jesus has already *become*. Become what? The Christ. And He's left us the Helper. He patiently waits for us, even though all creation is moaning and groaning for us to grow up and *get it* (Rom 8:22). Earth marriages are one of the ways that we become ready for marriage to the Lamb. It's on the job training; don't resist it!

In marriage, in this **triple dynamic** of *his becoming, her becoming and their (the marriage) becoming*, we travail. We travail in marriage because it is a *process*.

Consider a food processor. Do you think the vegetables that are being *processed* are enjoying being chopped, sliced, diced, pulverized, pureed, or whatever, to fit into the recipe that you are preparing? Processing hurts. Being changed from one thing to another can hurt a great deal unless **you love the cause more than your comfort.** *(They loved not their life unto death, Rev 12:11)--*, that is, they loved the *cause* more than the pain involved in the *process*. The process can be painful if it is forced, too drastic, or happens too quickly. And, the less God you have on board, the worse the process will feel. The less God-consciousness you have, the more you will resist. The more you resist, the longer the process will take and the more it will hurt.

Fortunately, God neither *processes* us too quickly, nor *over* processes. Humans do not have *processing* wisdom; therefore, we should never try to change anyone or *process* them into anything. Only God.

Just as God has created us in His own image and likeness, everything we would try to process, form, or create will be in *our* image, likeness or at least would go through our personal filtering system. How scary would your mate be if you were able to transform him or her into what **you** wanted him or her to be! *Eek!* You don't know what to do, how to change him or her, or when to stop (*but you may think you do*).

Over-processed hair looks and smells bad, and that's dead flesh. How much worse, the smell of crucifying *living* flesh. Don't touch it; let God do it! If you can wait until he/she is through with, or well into the *process* to marry, do that. If you cannot, or have not, brace yourself and pray.

Things I like about my mate:

1. _____
2. _____
3. _____

Things I can't stand about my mate:

1. _____
2. _____
3. _____
—

What will I do about it:

1. _____
2. _____
3. _____

If you didn't use all the space for Question 1, but need more space for Question 2, reconsider marriage to this particular person at this time. If already married, pray!

His Process

The wedded man is in the process of *becoming*. He is becoming the Husband. A Husband is one who has a Wife and treats her as Christ treats the Church.

How did Christ treat the Church? Very, very well. He provided the following (with modern examples).

1. Provision – Finances, financial security.
2. Intercession/prayer – Prays for his wife.
3. Exhortation – Encourages and inspires you.
4. Teaching – Teaches, patiently, lovingly.
5. Prophecy – Sees and sets the Marriage Vision.
6. Admonition – Warns, when necessary, but in Love.
7. Redemption – Ransoms, rescues from singleness, aloneness, and even from unforeseen troubles.
8. Sanctification – Washing by the water of the Word.
9. Sacrifice – Husband *prefers* the mate over himself.

10. Adoption – Accepts you into his family because you two make a brand-new family.
11. Justification – Believes you over others. ALWAYS.
12. Impartation of Righteousness – You can use his name with authority; you receive respect and perks, as if he is there, even when he's not.
13. Stewardship – He takes care of business, and manages well.
14. Healing – Prays for your health, lays hands on.
15. Comfort – touches, holds you.
16. Leading – Leads the family.
17. Setting order – As Jesus built the church, the husband sets marriage order.
18. Protection – Security, safety.
19. Feeding/nurturing – He feeds you both spiritual and natural food.
20. Had/used and ministered the Mind of Christ.
21. Walks in the Spirit – chooses the high road in times of crisis or decision.
22. Models Righteousness – is a role model for your family.
23. Works miracles and healings – by the Spirit of God.
24. Counsel – advises in truth and in Love.
25. Beauty for Ashes – turns bad into good.

No man is all of that, at the altar, on the wedding day. It is a formidable task, to become all that. But *Christ* is not Jesus' last name, it's His *anointing*. And Jesus Christ left anointing in the Earth for us because we certainly need it--, especially men who must walk the way He walked. Man, here is your confession and affirmation: *I can do all things through* (the) *Christ* (anointing) *which strengthens me. I receive and use the husbandman's anointing, daily; I need the husbandman's anointing.*

The average woman may not have considered all of what Christ did for the Church and all that a man has to *become* for his wife and family. Before she says, *I do,* she may not have considered any of it. But after, *I do,* she will think on it, because she, and the marriage need all of it.

Please note: *He's cute,* or *He's got a good sense of humor* is not on the list of what Jesus did for the Church.

My Mate Compares, *How*?

Considering how Christ treats the Church, place a check mark or an **X** by the characteristics listed on the previous page to see how your mate sizes up. Then think of those things that you or your mate have done or are currently doing that are Christ-like.

How can I (the husband) become more Christ-like…
more like Christ treated the Church?

_____

How can I (the Husband) strengthen my weaknesses?

_____

How can I (the Wife) help my husband be more Christ-
like *without getting on his nerves?*

_____

Hint: *Pray without ceasing,* (1 Thessalonians 5:17).

Her Process

The woman too, has to *become.* At the altar
she is a happy person (usually) in a beautiful dress
(also, usually.) That's it. She may already be some
of the things that the Church is supposed to be, but
she has not yet legally *become* or been any of those
things for her mate. Not yet--, except in her flesh;
so, she also has to *become.*

Just as there is a Christ anointing and the
Husbandman's anointing, (the anointing that
husbands must receive), there is also an anointing
for the Wife. Primarily, since she is called to be the
Helpmate, she receives of the *Helper's anointing.*
This is phenomenal because the Helper's anointing
can make a woman proficient at many things, at a
moment's notice. (Please note, I did not say that
she becomes the Holy Spirit, I said, *helper – lower*

case.) The fact that anyone must be, do, or *become* anything in the Earth, and they need an anointing to do it may mean that it is not necessarily going to be easy. With God all things are possible as long as you believe (Mark 9:23). The woman can also do all things through Christ. She uses the Wife's Anointing every day. Women, affirm yourself, daily.

Like the Church, the wife has to *become* these, as well as other things:

- **Glorious**. Glory only comes when something is broken down to its essence, down to its lowest common denominator. Man is spirit, when he looks and behaves as an anointed spirit, when you look like Christ, because that's what you were created for; that's glory, even if it's suffering, longsuffering or bearing your cross.
- **Spot-free**. Most can't even get their drinking glasses dishes spot-free, how much more difficult is it to get *flesh* spot-free? The Wife needs Jesus—big time.
- **Blemish free**. This may be difficult as a teenager, but as maturity approaches this is easier in the natural. Here, we mean spiritually spot, blemish, and –

- **Wrinkle free**. *Wrinkle free* means you must never stop learning and growing, else you age. Aging brings on wrinkles. Press on to the mark of the prize of the high calling in Jesus, (Php 3:14). Press forward. **Press** out the wrinkles!
- **Birth children**. The woman conceives and gives birth, just as in Jesus Christ, we are re-born and reared by the Spirit of God.
- **Trimming the Lamps**. She prepares and makes ready both spiritually, and naturally.
- **Nurturing**. Men have a role in nurturing as well, but women are considered the primary caregivers to infants and small children.

Some women are not called, anointed, or appointed to be mothers. As mothers they, themselves are stressed out and end up doing more harm than good. Pray. Ask the Lord if you are designed to be a mother before marrying anyone who expects you to be one. Having a baby to get a man or marrying to get a baby will produce a **child of your flesh.** Abraham and Hagar had a flesh child and so did others in the Bible. (David & Bathsheba's firstborn, Hosea & Gomer's children, et cetera.).

If you recall the situations, were not pleasant for the parents, children or any of the people involved. If God says, **"Yes,"** that you are called to be a mother, ask for the *mother's anointing* and for Wisdom to be a mother. Most people think it is something you learn. You can learn to act in any situation, and you can learn almost anything, but being a mother is different than learning mothering, or *acting* as though you're a mother. Acting mothers are picture perfect in public, especially in church. Their children have terrible home lives and childhoods. Bad mothering shows up (in the child) long after childhood.

- **Sanctuary**. The church provides Sanctuary for the lost, hungry, hurt, needy, widowed, poor and especially the unsaved. A man wants his home to be a sanctuary or haven of rest; he predominantly relies on the wife to make that happen.

Just as the church is not a sanctuary for sin, neither should your home be, for either spouse or your children. If you are not ready to face the reality of your own unrighteousness, wrongs, sins, don't get married. If married, 'fess up (repent) and get on with the business of living.

- **Providing Hope**. The Church provides Hope to a lost and dying generation as it reveals the manifold Wisdom of the mysteries of God to the world, (Eph 3:10).

Wives need and should pray for the gift of being able to give encouragement as many men suffer the opposite and sometimes become worn out or discouraged and may give up because of it.

- **Light**. Lights are not evident except in darkness. Bright lights take energy; brighter lights take more energy. Lights point in the direction of what they intend to light. The woman is as a light to the family as the Church is for the world. The Lord must tell her how to be what her family needs so they will be drawn to, warmed by, and comforted by it...*let us put on the armor of light,* (Rom 12:12c).

Rule 2: Agree to Become One

When you marry, you agree to become *one.* If you have no intentions of becoming *one spirit,* or in our human understanding, **one flesh** with your mate, do not marry him/her (Eph 5:31). The man must become the Husband as the woman becomes the Wife, at the same time the two of them come together to become a *new entity*: a married couple. It takes a process and if it were easy, the divorce rate would not be over 50% in and out of the Church. If it were easy vows that you promise to keep would not be necessary. To me, marriage is like agreeing to a survivor trip for 25, 40, 50 or more years. Yet, the objective is not to out-survive your mate, it is to work together so that *both* of you can survive as well as your children and your *children's* children. Can you do it?

Rule 3: Marriage Has Discipline

Marriage Has Disciplines, and it takes discipline to be married successfully and stay married. If you have no intention of practicing the Disciplines of Marriage; don't marry anyone. *Thank you, very much*. Many who eventually marry start out with what I call **Dating Discipline**, but the dating behavior has to transcend into **Marriage Discipline** for the marriage to work. When dating, you're polite, courteous, you don't stand your dates up, you call when you say you're going to call. Some men open some doors, some pay for dates. Some women say, *Thank you* when dates are over. Women fix themselves up and look nice for dates; men try to do that too-, many times they succeed.

But when the dating is over one or both, to a small or large degree throw their (usually self-enforced) **Dating Discipline** out the window and become to a small or large degree--, slobs. Hair curlers show up on her head, on hair that is now a different color at the roots than it was! Who is this woman? He didn't even know that she owned hair curlers! There are holes in his undershirts, socks, and boxers. BOXERS! She didn't even know he wore boxers and had told him that only old fuddy-duddies wore them. He used to be so neat and well-dressed. Anyway, the **Dating Discipline**, the same things that they both used to attract the other is all of a sudden gone. Either or both may be wondering if the other is house-broken or has any home training.

Common Marriage Disciplines are things such as: Behave as though you have some sense and have been exposed to at least a little of God's magnificent creation (world).

- Express common courtesy to your spouse. Speak when you come into the house or when you leave the building. *Marriage mystery* is fatiguing, not intriguing. Come correct.)
- How about: *"I'm going to the kitchen to get a glass of water; would you like one?"*
- Say, *"Good morning"*, when it's morning. Say, *"Good night,"* when it's night.
- **Common sense**. If you don't have any common sense, don't want any, or don't

plan to use what you already have, don't marry anybody.

Also, without Jesus, don't expect to suddenly get any common sense. If already married, you have no choice, *behave* as if you have sense. Seek sense. Learn. Find out how things are done in marriage. Read books on the subject. Get knowledge. Get understanding (Proverbs 4:7). Ask for Wisdom. God gives it liberally (James 1:5). learn your spouse, so at least you'll know the do's and don't of living married in the same house with your spouse (1Peter 3:7).

The first set of **Marriage Disciplines** come from the Shalt *Nots* --, all of them., every one of them. If you cannot at least walk in the *Shalt-Nots*, you are not ready for marriage. If you are not saved, marriage is really not designed for you. Marriage is a *spiritual* union, which requires two spiritually minded participants. The Shalt-Nots are commonly known as the Ten Commandments. In this book, **MARRIAGE ED.,** they can be known as the **Ten Commandments of Marriage**.

Rule 4: Shalt-Not I

Shalt *Not* I: Thou shalt have no other gods before me (Exodus 20:3).

Not only that, but thou also shalt not have any person, or thing before your mate.

Forsaking is a **Discipline of Marriage**. You do not only forsake when you're dating or on the wedding day; you forsake 24/7, preferring your mate, putting nothing before him or her for the entire term of your marriage, except God. (See also, **Rule 26**.)

God puts nothing before you; His mind is full of thoughts of you; do the same for your mate (Psalm 8:4). Can you imagine asking the Father for something, in Jesus' Name and Him responding, **"I'll get with you tomorrow or next month, right now, I am over here helping these sinners"?** —people with whom He is *not* in covenant! You wouldn't like that very much, would you? Neither would your spouse. *"I'll help you later, sweetie, right now I'm over here helping these people I'm NOT married to."* God first, self, spouse, friends, and then strangers.

Do you have anything that your mate has to take a back seat to? (Refer to the list below.)

Finances?_____ Ex's? _____ Job? _____

Children? _____ Dog, Cat, Iguana, any pet? _____

Car, Truck or Motorcycle? _____ Sports? _____

Friends? _____ Mall? _____ Other?

Are you willing to change that? _____

Would you give up any of the above? _____

Which one or ones, and what would it take? _____

What things do you feel your mate has put ahead of you?

Can the two of you discuss it without a huge blow-up?

Rule 5: Shalt-Not II

Shalt Not II: Thou shalt not make unto thee any graven image, or any likeness of anything that is in heaven above, or that is in the Earth beneath, or that is in the water under the Earth:

Thou shalt not bow down thyself to them, nor serve them: for I the LORD thy God am a jealous God, (Exodus 20:4-5).

God says don't make images or likenesses of Him. As well, this Shalt-*Not* goes back to *processing*. Do not set **your** image in your mind of what your spouse should be when they finish the *process*; else you will set a false image of your mate, and ultimately have false expectations. Your mate is *fearfully and wonderfully made* (Psalm 139:14) how can you fathom it all? Your image will be based on your desires and imaginations, your past, unhealed hurts, unresolved issues, unmet needs, your own lusts. Verse 5: *Bowing down and worshipping them,* means *worshipping* the **false image** of your spouse – what you wish (or even pray) that he/she would be or become. When you rehearse and imagine over and again, even in your mind, that is bowing down and worshipping the image--, not the Creator or what the **Creator** says your mate should be. This is idolatry and disobedience.

God is not pleased, and you will at least get on the mate's nerves, at most cause him/her to feel rejected. You two will have at least frequent fights or all out marital war.

Begin to get **God's image** of your mate in your mind; accept him/her as is but work toward what God says he/she should be. I promise you, that's what you want your mate to do for you.

You do not *own* your spouse, he/she is a gift from God that you help or steward. When a man starts to look like the image of what his wife wants him to be, it's called *henpecked*. When a woman starts to look like the image of what her husband says she should be, it is said that she is a *kept* woman and/or that he is *controlling*. If you plan to henpeck or control your spouse, (both are control, and control is witchcraft), don't get married. If the henpecking and controlling work, and you consider yourself successful, you won't appreciate, love, or respect him or her anymore. And if it doesn't "work", you'll both be frustrated.

Ultimately, referring back to **MARRIAGE ED., Rule #1**: If you could change the person you married into what you want him or her to be, (*thank God you can't*) you won't be attracted to, or want him or her anymore.

If you are married, make some real assessments of your situation. Married or single, answer the following:

Who is my mate?

Do I really see him/her as they are?

Do I imagine or daydream about my mate being different?

Do I fantasize about him/her, wishing he/she would be like someone else?

(*Vain things, vain thoughts,* (Ps 2:1, Acts 4:25 and Ps 119:113)

How does God see my mate?

Can I, do I see him/her as *God* does? How?

How would I feel to know that my mate is only *tolerating* certain things about me and secretly wants to change them or is fantasizing or comparing me to others, real or virtual?

Casting down imaginations, and every high thing that exalteth itself against the knowledge of God, and bringing into captivity every though to the obedience of Christ; (2 Cor 10:5)

Rule 6 Shalt-Not III

Shalt Not* III: Thou shalt not take the name of the LORD thy GOD in vain;** for the LORD will not hold him guiltless that taketh His name in vain, (Exodus 20:7).   If   you don't respect, honor, and esteem the Name of the Lord God, don't try to make it in any His spiritual covenants, especially marriage. If you don't recognize the identity of God, His ***deity will surely escape you.

Taking your spouse's name in vain? No one wants to be called *out of their name. Let no corrupt communication flow out of your mouth, but minister Grace to the hearer,* (Eph 4:39). If you do not know how to talk to your partner, don't marry him or her, even if he/she puts up with it.

How to **speak edification and life** is only ***spiritually*** captured. Your mate needs and deserves edifying conversation and expects it. Speaking kindly to and of one another, in love (agape) is part of the reasonable service of marriage. As well, it is ***a Marriage Discipline***. In addition, where do you think our mate will get this kind of conversation? Who will speak positively into his/her life, if not you? Boss? Friends? Relatives? Whether or not you trust that anyone else is encouraging or supporting your mate, it should primarily **be you**.

Rule 7 Shalt-Not IV

Shalt Not IV: Remember the sabbath day, to keep it holy, (Exodus 20:8).

Remember God's sabbaths and marriage *sabbaths* are special, set-aside days in life. If you are not one to remember them and have no system or help in doing so, you are asking for trouble. If you acknowledge special days in your marriage, it may not go well for you. The Word says *it is better to marry than to burn* (1 Cor 7:9), if you forget your spouse's birthday, anniversary, you may make them burning mad. If you are prone to get into this kind of trouble, get help--, a calendar, planner, secretary, friend--, put the dates in your cell phone. A personal florist can keep your special dates on file. If you know your anniversary is in April, give your spouse a gift, card or whatever on the first of the anniversary month. Don't risk missing it. When you love and honor someone, you don't forget the special days.

A fellow I met once invited me on a special date--, it was his birthday! He had told me what day his birthday was when we had met several weeks earlier and had chosen to share the day with me! But I hadn't remembered. He was looking for a wife, and needless to say, I had forgotten his birthday. So, I was **not** the wife he was looking for.

Rule 8   Shalt-Not V

Shalt Not V: **Honour thy father and thy mother**: that thy days may be long upon the land which the LORD thy god giveth thee, (Exodus 20:12).

As you *become* in your marriage, you and your spouse may become parents (father/mother). You may begin to call each other by those titles instead of Husband, Wife, or by your given names, to model it for your children. When you honor one another personally and in the office of Husband and the office of Wife you will probably have occasion to honor the *offices* of Father and Mother as you teach honor to your children, but also because this commandment is the first *with promise.*

If keeping this command has promise, not keeping it has the opposite effect, no promise, no blessing, perhaps instead, cursing. Listen closely: If you, as an individual have not honored, or have dishonored your own Father or Mother at any time since you were born into the Earth, you have brough the Curse of the Law into your life. Now, you may see why some negative things have happened to you that you may not have understood, such as poverty or sickness.

If you're under the Curse, when you marry, you bring that curse right into your new relationship, home, family and pass it on to your kids if it is not properly dealt with (repented of). The same is true of your spouse. So, if you both have rebelled against your (godly) parents and eloped, when forbidden to marry, you're just asking for trouble. You are living doubly under the Curse. Both of you must repent, or watch your lives not go well in the Earth, not have *length of days* – for you or your children.

Prayer: Father, in the Name of Jesus, I repent of having dishonored _____. I turn from that behavior in the Name of Jesus and ask You to forgive me and cleanse me of all iniquity for this transgression. Show me how to respect, honor and love _____ (my parent or parents, no matter how they treat me, or have treated me). I choose to obey Your laws and precepts over how I feel. I choose to honor parents and authority figures to bring power to my prayers, success in life and glory to Your Name. In Jesus' Name. Amen.

See also, **Rule 85,** *Children Obey Your Father & Mother.*

Rule 9   Shalt-Not VI

Shalt Not **VI: Thou shalt not kill** (Exodus 20:13).

There are any number of ways you can kill any number of things. If you have thoughts of killing, murder, and the like, it is best not to marry until you have received deliverance from those oppressive thoughts and intents. A youth who pulls the wings off flies, to watch them suffer and slowly die should not be ignored. Did you do this as a child? Repent of having murderous thoughts. Do you become enraged and plan vengeance and harm on a perpetrator or suspected perpetrator? Are you full of thoughts or plans of vengeance, retaliation, or payback toward human beings (not speaking of spiritual warfare here)? Repent of murderous thoughts. Have you ever wished or "prayed" that someone would die? That's witchcraft. Repent.

The way you speak to your mate can kill his or her spirit, the marriage, or the *Spirit of the Marriage*. Repenting of the marriage, repenting of ever having met the spouse, especially **to** your spouse, repenting of asking him or her to marry you, or his or her proposal--, these are all marriage killers. If you are guilty of any of this, or anything like this, you're potentially a marriage murderer. Repent of murderous thoughts and words.

Dealing unjustly with money, especially other people's – namely God's – robbing Him in the tithes and offerings can kill the finances of your home. Repent.

Do I have murderous thoughts?

_____

What sparks those thoughts?

_____

Do not suffer as a murderer... (1 Peter 4:15). Whether you are married or unmarried, if you have murderous thoughts, you need deliverance, repentance and probably counseling. Don't be ashamed; get the help you deserve.

Prayer

Father, in the Name of Jesus, I repent for any sin against You. I repent of murder and thoughts of murder. You are Merciful, Kind, Gracious and forgiving. I must confess as sin any and all murderous, killing, and destructive thoughts and ask You to cleanse them from me. Take them far away from me, Lord and the iniquity associated with them.

Remember my sins no more. Forgive me for words and word curses that have killed or nearly killed my marriage, my mate's honor, self-esteem, self-respect, or the Spirit of the Marriage. I renounce and revoke those murderous words and cover them with the Blood of Jesus. You are a Covenant-making and Covenant-keeping God; make me like You--, like Your dear Son; help me to keep Covenant, speaking life into my marriage and other godly relationships. Help me to speak life into my mate instead of death and defeat. Minister to my heart, Lord that I may be more like You and less in the flesh.

I repent of murder, killing, murderous thoughts and intent. You forgave Moses and David, both for murder, and You have even loved and forgiven mankind for putting Your Son on the Cross. Father, forgive me, send complete deliverance now, that I may be made whole. In place of the *spirit of murder*, fill me

with Your Holy Spirit and with Love. In Jesus'
Name. Amen.

Rule 10   Shalt-Not VII

Thou shalt not commit adultery (Ex 20:14,
Proverbs 6:29-32).

There are all kinds of adultery: emotional
adultery, physical adultery, and spiritual adultery.
When you have committed adultery mentally it's
still adultery to God; to God the deed is done, If
you can't be true in your mind and thought life to
God, what makes you think you can be true to
your spouse? If your Christian walk is slack,
shabby, or shaky it is not wise to enter into
spiritual covenant with a living, visible person
especially if they are shaky, if they are weak, too.
Seek help.

If you have adulterous thoughts and are full of
lust or trying to repress lust and lustful thoughts
all the time, or worse, you may not be trying to
repress lust at all, you won't be a faithful partner. If
you are acting on these lusts and then trying to
hide it, or not hide it, don't marry anybody. Do not
make your mate try to satisfy you to fix your
sexual and addictive problems.

*Submit to God resist the devil and he will flee from
you.* Without God's intervention and spiritual

deliverance, you cannot overcome lust; and when you fail while trying to do it all on your own, you will invariably blame your spouse for not being attractive enough, willing enough, fun enough, *built* enough, or slim enough. Adultery can be a real sharp weapon for killing (a marriage), which is the aforementioned **Shalt Not VI.**

Rule 11   Shalt-Not VIII

Shalt Not VIII: **Thou shalt not steal** (Exodus 20:15).

Stealing is a precursor to murder. If you're not an honest person and do not/cannot deal honestly with money such as, tithes, offerings or other peoples' money, don't marry anybody.

There's help for every one of these Shalt-Nots: Salvation. When you get saved the Spirit of God helps you keep His commandments. So I suppose I'm really saying if you're not saved don't enter into the *spiritual* union called marriage expecting a favorable outcome.

Do not suffer as a thief (1Peter 4:15b).

Recommended: ***Among Some Thieves*** by this author.

Rule 12   Shalt-Not IX

Thou shalt not bear false witness against thy neighbor, (Ex 20:16).

Lying is a precursor to stealing I suppose when God sent the Laws down, He gave them in this order to help us know how NOT to do the thing that He had just commanded us not to do. God just broke it down for us; we have no excuses

See also, **Rule 30,** *Put Away Lying,* and **Rule 20,** *Speak the Truth in Love.*

Rule 13   Shalt-Not X

Shalt *Not* X: Thou shalt not covet thy neighbor's house, thou shalt not covet thy neighbor's wife, nor his manservant, nor his maidservant nor his ox, nor his donkey, nor anything that is in my neighbor's (Exodus 20:17).

Thou shalt not covet ...anything. Coveting is the precursor to lying, stealing, murder, and idolatry. If you covet, that really means you're not satisfied with what the Lord has given you. That shows that you either have no faith for what else He will give you, or you are too impatient. Coveting is related to envy and jealousy; they are works of the flesh and works of the flesh do not work in the spiritual union and work called marriage if you need to get past coveting it would be best to wait until after you do to get married.

The Ten Commandments is for sinners. It is the Law, and it brings man to the knowledge and conviction that he isn't saved. When he realizes he can't obey those 10 things without divine help, he should seek God. There are many other guides, statutes, precepts, and even commandments in the New Testament to help *saved* people refine our Christian walk, fulfill the Word, and acquire the promises of God. (See **Rule 58**.)

Rule 14 The New Commandment

Jesus gave a "New Commandment" (John 15:9-13, 1 Peter 4:8) *A new commandment I given to you that you love one another as I have loved you and you also love one another. By this show all men know that you are my disciples if you have love one to another,* (John 13:24-35).

This commandment fulfills all the OT Commandments, refines and more clearly defines man as a disciple of the Lord.

If you are not ready to love your *significant* other your intended who is your primary *one another*, the one with whom you *become one*, don't marry. You need to know for sure that your mate can love you (*agape*, unconditional love) before saying, *I do*. One way to know this is to observe if your mate can *agape* other people. If you are dating or married to someone who **_only_** loves you, and hates everyone else, **both** of you have problems.

If married you must offer unconditional love to your mate, no matter what he or she does to you; it's a law of God. Even if your mate is wrong, wrong, wrong God will avenge all disobedience when you remain obedient to His Word, (2 Corinthians 10:6). *Agape* is a choice. It is an act of your will, not your emotions. See **Rule 17, Bear Fruit: *Agape* Love.**

Those were the Shalt Nots. They are the basics for Christian life anyway, and you know you must be a Christian to have a Christian marriage.

MARRIAGE ED. now must go deeper into how to be married and the things you need to do, be willing to do, and **be** to make your marriage better.

Rule 15 Walk Worthy

Walk worthy of the Office of Husband or Wife. Husband or Wife are not just names they are *Offices* with a title, authority, rights, privileges, responsibility, and accountability to each other and to God, (Ephesians 4:1).

Office Title: Husband

Authority _____

Rights _____

Privileges _____

Husband's responsibilities and *to whom* is he responsible? _____

To whom is the Husband accountable? _____

Office Title: Wife

Authority _____

Rights _____

Privileges _____

What are the wife's responsibilities and *to whom is* she responsible? _____

To whom is the wife accountable? _____

Hints: (Genesis 1:2b, Psalms 8, Ephesians 1:6-12, Eph 5:21-31, 1 Peter 3).

Take this quiz with your mate then compare notes if you are still speaking to one another afterward, take the quiz below together.

Office Title: Child

Authority: _____

Rights _____

Privileges _____

What are the child's responsibilities? _____

To whom is the child responsible? _____

To whom is the child accountable? _____

Hint: The child is not equal with or above either parent. He/she is not equal with the mother or the father and is certainly not **over** either parent at any time; that is dysfunctional, (1Kings 3:7, Galatians 4:1-2).

Rule 16 Walk in the Spirit

Walk in the Spirit. Even if you are distracted by your mate and marriage situations you must stay in the Spirit. Staying in the Spirit for 20 minutes during worship on Sunday morning is hard enough for too many but that's not what I'm talking about staying in the Spirit means you have to be willing to go low you have to choose the lowliness when you have a choice as well as meekness longsuffering forbearing one another goodness unity righteousness peace and truth choose to walk in the Spirit.

Instead, walking by your own understanding or in the flesh will dim your Wisdom and understanding. Flesh-walking makes you ignorant and your heart blind (Ephesians 4:18).

The mind of Christ (1 Corinthians 2:16) is on one accord with God and is like minded with Him. This mind is compassionate, offers exhortation and comfort, has a servant's heart, prefers the other marriage partner, is obedient to God and authority even unto death does not strive with others for operates in humility and lowliness is not on an ego trip or self-exalting.

At the same time the mind of Christ is balanced to think it is not robbery to be equal with God after having been humbled and then exalted by God, (Ephesians 4:9-10).

Be renewed in the spirit of your mind, (Eph 4:1-3, Galatians 5:16-25).

How to Walk in the Spirit

Walking in the Spirit is a choice when a crossroad presents to make a choice. You have to learn recognize when a decision must be made. Take yourself off automatic and evaluate your life *as* you are living it

- Use discernment to know that a choice needs to be made have you ever stepped away from a situation and said to yourself I should have done or said this or that or I wished I done this that or the other. To walk in the Spirit you must be able to evaluate a situation *while yet in it*. In God, you still can go back and make corrections and apologies and make things right with people.

- Know the word of God and know what choice to make.

Initially when you begin choosing the spirit over your flesh it won't feel good. Your flesh man will scream for you to do the exact opposite of what God says to do. If it feels good to your flesh is usually not God. Your flesh is at war with God. At first spirit choices will feel like death because they are death to your flesh. Over time your life choices will begin to feel like life.

Jesus chose life for us but it felt like death, and it was death to *His* flesh but He lives now and we also have life choosing life will bring life to your life and life to your marriage

Learn or at least become well acquainted with Deuteronomy, Chapters 28 through 30.

The following are good examples of choosing life instead of death choosing God instead of flesh each right choice bears godly life-giving marriage building the Fruit of the Spirit.

Rule 17   Bear Fruit

Bear the Fruit of the Spirit, (John 15:8-16b, Ephesians 4:2, 5, 9). Walking in the Spirit is tough enough for the average anybody but to bear fruit, and fruit that remains you've got to stay in the Spirit at least *several seasons* at a time. Most fruit trees need three seasons to begin to bear fruit and right then that may mean that the average situation that you go through in your marriage that requires your walking in the Spirit and last as long as 9 to 12 months or more depending on you and your spouse's responses and reactions to it. Also, only **mature** plants bear fruit.

Lowliness (Ephesians 4:2, Colossians 3:12.)

How low can you go is a question answered by your response to the following questions how high is your building? How high do you want your building to be? How deep is your foundation? Building depth is commensurate with building height. If you want a very tall building, you need a very deep foundation. How deep does the foundation need to be that's how low you must go. For low-rise building you only need a shallow foundation. How low you can go is determined by how high your building is supposed to be. How long you can endure loneliness and wait for what the Lord has planned for you since before the foundation of the world?

If you want Heaven, You must be willing to go to hell; Jesus had to.

How much Fruit do you want? Deeper roots equal more fruit. How much anointing do you want? How near to God do you want to be? Then you must know Him and His suffering. Christ first descended then ascended (Eph 4:8-10).

In the Lord, taking the high ground means taking the road of lowliness not being puffed up and agreeing quickly with your mate your natural mind probably cannot process this. This is not a natural process--, this is spiritual keep your natural mind out of it (Ephesians 4:2-3). When you also, as Christ did, descend you will ascend far above all the heavens to rule and rest in dominion, (Ephesians 4:10). If you've always got to be right choosing pride instead of loneliness and humility you will make a horrible spouse.

If you want your prayers heard, drop pride, (Proverbs 16:18) if your mate is or you believe/perceive that they are prideful get married after counseling. If married, you know if you have a puffed-up spouse or not if you're the puffed up one you probably don't even realize it. Pray ask God to help you so you can stop tormenting your spouse and get on with the business of *becoming one* and living. Must you always be right and have the last word? That's pride. Can you let the other person win the argument for the sake of peace even if they're not *as* right as you are if it's a non-life and death situation? Can you do this, while not using deception? If so, that's lowliness.

Meekness

Lowliness has humility and Meekness in common (Col 3:12) with it. If you are not able to be Meek toward God that may be an indication that you also cannot show Meekness to your mate. Meekness is necessary for submission and general pleasantness. For best results, yield to the Spirit of God to produce this Fruit in you before you marry. Married, or not, opportunities come up all day long to help you develop Meekness; what will you do with those opportunities, take the flesh or the Spirit walk?

Why do I have to have Fruit of the Spirit, anyway? Because God says to. We are the trees (Isa 61:30) Jesus curses trees that do not bear fruit.

People in need of fruit will come up to you so you can minister to them.

In marriage, you need something to feed and nurture your spouse – Fruit. And you need Fruit to sweeten things up so your mate will be able to stand you. Example: Choose your mate's feelings over your own, that's Meekness.

Longsuffering

Longsuffering is not just suffering for a long time; it is suffering well, (Col 3:12). Many times, suffering well, especially in Lowliness will allow you to go lower, which means you will eventually ascend higher. Suffering well causes the suffering time to be shortened. Longsuffering means you don't fall apart or try to blame everyone in the entire world, your mate, or God every time or any time things don't go well or as you wish them to go on in life. It also means that when very real challenges come up you walk worthy and look like a real Christian as you *go through,* or suffer is a witness to many, saved and unsaved. Further, suffering well helps your mate to be able to *stand you.* If a piece of burnt toast throws your whole day (or week!) off, no matter whose fault it is, you don't suffer well. Don't marry yet.

If you are already married, as the Lord to help you so you don't become repulsive or beyond help.

Chronically no having necessary vitamins and minerals will adversely affect your physical health. There are many nutrients, including vitamins and minerals in **fruit.** When you don't have spiritual Fruits or access to them, your spiritual health may be adversely affected and spiritual/emotional strongholds may be built up--, just to cope.

Suffering well, yes you will suffer in life, and also in marriage, because it is not all peaches and cream--, releases an anointing for use in this life and it earns you an Eternal Crown, (1Pe2:19-25) *Example: Not Longsuffering: Spouse is acting up, complain to anyone who will listen. Longsuffering: Tell Jesus; pray, shut up and believe God.*

Forbearing One Another in Love

If you are not willing, prepared, ready, or able to put up with your spouse no matter what he/she does or doesn't do, don't get married right now, (Eph 4:2-3, Col 3:13). Forbearance requires unconditional love. If you don't have *agape* toward your mate, do you have it toward *anyone*? Do you just act like a nice person in public? Example: Not Forbearing: *"I'm not taking anymore of your stuff."* Forbearing is putting up with your mate, realizing he/she has to, or will have to put up with you, and is in the process of so doing.

- **Goodness** (Col 3:12)

Most of the Fruit of the Spirit is modeled and shown to you by your parents in your childhood home. People with really bad, unreconciled childhoods make the worst marriage partners. Sometimes they never "partner" they just associate with their mates. Too many times they live their lives in Pain Cliques (soul ties) with their also wounded, adult siblings who have (the same) horrible, unreconciled childhoods, (Eph 5:9 and 1Peter 3:8-9). Generally speaking, if you have not been treated with Goodness from childhood or have not been healed by the Love of Jesus Christ, since childhood, since you met Him, you are probably a miserable sort and will make a spouse miserable. Except for Jesus, wouldn't we all? You surely don't need an example for Good vs. Bad, do you?

- *Agape* **Love** (John 15:9-13; Col 3:14)

Until you're able to love God and all of His creation unconditionally, don't get married, (Eph 4:3). If you've been trained in conditional love by controlling parents, that's all you know. That's all you will ever know--, except for Jesus. A person cannot change that for you and take away the real (and perceived) pain you feel. Only Jesus. Don't marry expecting your mate to love the pain of an unreconciled childhood, divorce, unmet needs, unhealed hurts, and unresolved issues out of you. Yes, you really hurt, that's why there is a special anointing for the broken hearted, wounded and captive (Isa 61:1) but if you won't let Jesus fix it, how do you think your spouse, a mere human will fix it?

Fix if **first**. Allow Jesus to fix it; then get married. If you are already married: let Jesus fix it, then live! Example: I love you if or when you do this or that. Or unconditional love: I love you anyway, no matter what. (See **Rules 14, 20, and 47**)

If we love one another, God dwelleth in us, and his love is perfected in us. 1 John 4:12b

- **Unity; Keep the Unity of the Spirit**

Keep the Unity of the Spirit? Yeah. Don't break up the Spirit; let it flow. Let it have its way in your life and marriage. Let it flow through you 24/7;

don't be one way sometimes and another way another time; this quenches and grieves the Holy Spirit. Keep the unity of the Spirit by letting the same Spirit flow through you that flows through your mate, that flows through your marriage and home. One Spirit--, the same Spirit, (Eph 4:3, 13).

Keep the Spirit of the Marriage which is Unity, *becoming one*, communion, trust, *agape* Love, one-another and Purpose, (Eph 4:2-3)-- determination and reaching goals all come of unity for this cause, unity shall a man leave his father and mother, (Ephesians 5:31). The spirit of marriage is being ever mindful of the cause of your marriage. Purpose and destiny. Cause overrides emotions, hurt feelings and petty arguments. Remember your vows? You made them because of the **cause**. When the people are one, there's something that will be withheld from them, (Genesis 11:6).

Once again. Marriage is spiritual. A spiritual covenant only made kept developed and becoming fully formed. Full grown by the Spirit else is flesh, conflict, or counterfeit.

Righteousness. (Matthew 6:33, Ephesians 5:9, 1 Peter 3:8-9, Isaiah 64:6)

None of us have any righteousness if you don't know that you are definitely not ready to be married. Your own righteousness will get on your mates' nerves very quickly. Jesus is our righteousness until you put on the righteousness of Christ. You will not be well tolerated by your spouse and God won't pay much attention to you either. The eyes of the Lord are over the righteous, (1 Peter 12:14) married or not, do not rely on your own righteousness. It is as filthy rags, example. *I'm right, I'm always right.*

If you just can't stand to be wrong, that is self-righteousness and pride. (See Rule 2:9.)

Peace (Ephesians 2:14 Colossians 3:15.)

The bond of peace is to keep unity in marriage. Jesus is our peace. He broke down the middle wall of partition and drew us to Himself, becoming our peace. He is the only way. You can keep the peace of marriage in unity is by peace by Jesus Christ. Are you doing your own thing or are you moving in the Spirit of unity in the marriage?

Rule 18 Use Grace, Give Grace

Use grace; give grace. Until you know what Grace is and how to use it, do not get married, (Ephesians 4:8-10.)

Do you verbally or nonverbally keep account of wrongs done? That's supervision or management, something you do on your job; that is not love. Do you vow that the marriage partner will pay for wrongs done? That's not grace. And it's not love. Grace forgives, forgets, and blesses instead of curses or requiring payment for wrongs done.

The Word says *Let your speech be always with grace, seasoned with salt, that you might know how to answer. Every man,* (Colossians 4:6). Of course, there it is speaking of telling an unbeliever what you believe in, but grace is useful in your daily life, especially in your marriage and your children. Grace does not mean to be a doormat; it means give as God would, as He would forgive quickly, easily. Offer much mercy instead of demanding justice, give grace generously. Grace is receiving good when you should be receiving bad. Giving Grace is giving reward in the place of doling out punishment. Of course, we don't reward bad behavior, especially in children, But when repentance has truly come, God has a very forgiving heart toward man.

Grace is a power. Power comes from God. So God gives you the grace to minister the proper words and attitude to those with whom you interact, namely your spouse.

Edify and administer Grace to your spouse. Empower your mate with the words you speak. If you can't, won't or are not ready to do that, do not get married. If you are already married, you must put on Grace immediately, (Ephesians 4:29).

Rule 19   Use Your Spiritual

Use your spiritual gifts for your marriage. What are the spiritual gifts for? To keep order in the church and home as everyone moves in their own gifting and does not try to imitate, anointing, or gifting. This way success is assured and frustration and defeat ae circumvented. Also using the Gifts in the home will help you and your mate mature and make your ministry work, which is in this case your marriage, your **cause**. Using those gifts will assist you in *becoming one* with your mate to cause the husband to look more like Christ. And the wife to look more like the Church. It will help you both stand in the doctrine you know and not be tossed to and fro. It will help you not be deceived (Ephesians 5:6).

Two important gifts of the marriage are stewardship, usually on the husband's part and hospitality, usually on the wife's part, (1 Pe 4:9-10).

What are your top two or three spiritual gifts?

What are your mate's, top two or three spiritual gifts? Do they correlate? How?

Rule 20   Speak the Truth, in Love

Speak the truth to one another in love, (Ephesians 4:2-5,9, Colossians 3:16.) If you cannot or will not speak the truth to your mate, you do not need to get married. If your mate cannot *receive* truth because he or she is too sensitive, don't marry him or her unless you want spats, fights, and tests on the level of Job's. *Oversensitivity* is caused by hurts, offense, rejection, selfishness, self-centeredness, pride, and acute and chronic combinations of the aforementioned. There is help and deliverance for them all.

Lack of or poor communication is a main cause of failed marriages. Marriages that do not have regular truth-in-love conversations become comatose; eventually, no one is speaking to anyone. Communication is two-way; you must talk to *and* listen to your mate, daily.

Truth. (Ephesians 5:9, 1Peter 3:8-9.)

Know the truth, speak the Truth, walk in Truth, seek the Truth, and get the Truth in you.

Speaking the Truth with the love Jesus loves us with is an important for growth. He cares for who we are, how we feel, and that we continue to grow. *Agape* is of the will, not of the emotions. No matter what your mate does or doesn't do, you still love him or her. Do not shut down after you hear the Truth. The Truth in love may come with conviction but never condemnation. (Also, Rules 12,20, and 30.)

Rule 21   Fit Together

Fit together, find out how you and your mate fit together. How you fit physically is immaterial, although that's what people try out, and get in the most trouble about. The other *fits* are most important: spiritually, in purpose, intellectually, and emotionally.

Look for what's right about your mate instead of what's wrong. Look for how you can compliment and complement, not compete with one another.

If you made or you are not able to find anything that's right in one another, or if you tend to dwell on what's wrong with one another, don't get married. If you have or are a critical faultfinding mate, get help; this is not God's best.

Hey, try this:

- Make a list of all the things you appreciate about your spouse. Think on those things.
- Tell your spouse or send him or her card, note, email, or text from time to time affirming him or her.
- Tomorrow, find something new and wonderful about your mate.
- Tell him or her.
- Repeat.

If you can't find anything or think of anything good on your own, ask someone who really knows your mate. A great person to ask is God. Pray. Ask God to show you or send someone who knows complimentary things about your mate. A best friend or your mate's mother *may* be good choices, but not always. If God loves your mate, you need to do the same.

If God can't stand your mate, don't marry him or her.

Now that you know who your mate is and as you are both *becoming* one, you must figure out how you fit together. Don't forget the world's dynamic, you are alive, your marriage is dynamic--, your *fit* may change from time to time. Ask yourselves these questions:

What does each supply to the whole?

_____

What does each bring to the marriage spiritually first, then in other ways?

_____

Be specific, not general.

Rule 22   Increase

Increase in your marriage, (Ephesians 2:21, 4:16).

What does *increase* look like in your marriage?

How can you increase your marriage in love?

A marriage that is *fitly joined together* with each of the members of the union in his or her place will show, *increase.* **Increase** is one of the ways you know the marriage is joined properly and sanctioned by God.

How can your marriage fit together better?

_____

Rule 23   Access the Mind of Christ

Access and use the Mind of Christ, (Ephesians 4:17, Colossians 3:3-16, 1 Peter 4:1-2). Your soul has a mind, emotions and will. The mind of a man is base and often greatly influenced by the emotions and flesh, thinking on and pursuing things that seem to be satisfying to the emotions or pleasing to the flesh. Those base things will never prosper you or your marriage.

The mind of Christ is accessed by your spirit, connecting with the Spirit of God to give you Wisdom, guidance, truth, peace and help you make decisions, (Proverbs 20:27). This is the Mind you need to use to be successful in marriage. It is accessed by walking in the Spirit, communing with God, prayer, worship, fasting and other disciplines, as well as Biblical meditation.

In order to properly get and use the Mind of Christ, you must at least be acquainted with the Word, *a workman that need not be ashamed,* (2 Timothy 2:15) and know God's voice when He speaks to you, (John 10:4). ***Get Wisdom, say to Wisdom, thou art my sister. Understanding, my kinswoman,*** (Proverbs 7:4, Col 3:16).

Rule 24   Be Likeminded

Be like minded (1 Peter 3:8, 4:1). Start out likeminded. Like many people, appreciate, pursue, and keep like values. Opposites attract. But unless God says so do not marry person who's very opposite in the way they think and do things. If honest, don't marry a liar. If you eat right and exercise, don't marry a lazy slob. If you're saved, don't marry a sinner, and et cetera.

Rule 25   No Flesh

No flesh. Put away the works of the flesh, especially lasciviousness, lust, and uncleanness. When you marry, quit flirting, winking, the little touches, coy smiles, cute repartee, revealing outfits, and soaking in cologne to get the opposite sex's attention. Those are many of the *old man's* toys. The old man's toys are tools of expressing sexual craving, depravity, lewdness, and enticement. If not ready to put away the old man's toys and playthings do not get married. Of course, some try to use these tricks to get their mate more interested or jealous to get more attention from their mate. This is dangerous, stupid, and ungodly.

If you have seen so much filth that you are no longer sensitized to it, if your conscience is so seared that you don't care if you do right or wrong, don't marry anyone. Marriage is a *spiritual* union, I remind you, (Ephesians 4:19). Flesh marriages don't work because there's always *more* flesh, better flesh, younger flesh, more muscular flesh. If you say, *I don't know much else, I know I like his* ____ *or her* ____. *(looks or anything related to sex)*, that is all flesh.

Mortify your flesh, (Colossians 3:5). Stop letting your flesh run the show. Don't feed cravings and addictions, especially lewd and defiled ones.

If you let your *child* run your house, you won't have a house very long. Flesh is like a child, don't let it run anything. (See Rule 28, and Rule 54.)

Rule 26   Forsake Others

Forsake All Others (Heb 13:5). If you choose marriage, be ready to *forsake. Forsaking* is giving up things that mean or have meant something to you: old girl/boyfriends, photos, keepsakes from the 1995 State Fair with JimBo, love letters, poems, his letter jacket, nice jewelry, even the pricey stuff--, forsake it. Not only the person and the personal relationship, but the *stuff* from the relationship(s) has got to go. (Not school yearbooks, but the exclusive dating stuff should be removed.)

Things that come from a cherished person, from a romantic relationship have memories and emotions attached to them; memories and emotions are part of the **soul**, and your mate can sense your distraction in his or her soul. If you are married and there's uneasiness in your home, get the previous relationship idols OUT! Gifts, cards, books, sweaters, socks. You can't remain best buddies with your Ex's mother/family and expect your marriage to prosper. Respect your mate.

When you got saved, you didn't keep the stuff from your previous relationship with the world, did you?

If you have been married before, get a new home when you remarry. Or get **everything** out of your house that your Ex, put, bought, chose for you, used together--, from linens to dishes, bath towels, draperies, furniture, pots and pans! EVERYTHING! Then watch peace and harmony come into your home. Yes, God is bigger than all this; but are you praying? (See Rule 4, 15, Rule 53.)

Rule 27   Cleave to Your Mate

Cleave To Your Mate. Husband: Leave your father and mother and be joined to your wife, so that two will *become* **one flesh** (Eph 5:31). The Bible says the man will leave and cleave to his wife. Maybe this is harder for the man than the woman because it had to be written for the man, twice in the Bible (also, Gen 2:24). You're married? Stop running to mom/dad for everything; be a grown up.

Some Husbands have to also *leave* their **siblings**.

Separate. Individuate to become **whole** in the Lord and then become *one* in your marriage. Many unsuccessful marriages ae that way, because of one or both mate's over attachment or improper attachment to a relative (or friend). So, they may be emotionally and spiritually unavailable for marriage to their marriage partner. Sounds weird? It is.

One definition of *cleave* is to penetrate or pierce. Another is to *adhere to, cling to* and be *faithful to*. The Bible says that cleave means, *to cling to, abide fast, follow close,* and *catch by pursuit*. Are you doing that? Are you planning to do that? No? Then don't marry anyone.

If you are already married, you'd better get to it. I tease my husband by saying, I will stick up under you. I love to nestle in that place where I probably came from by his ribs. Now that I know that it's biblical, I'm going to do it all the more, and let him *pursue me until he catches me*! (See Rule 81, and Rule 142.)

Rule 28   Put Off the Old Man

Put Off the Old Man and former conversation which is deceitful and full of lust (Ephesians 4:24). Remember marriage is a *spiritual* union and spiritual people must be in it, working it to make it successful. Before you were saved you thought on and talked about the things of the world which amounted to your own lust--, things that appealed to your flesh, your comfort, and your idea of fun. You can still have fun, but fun in the Lord doesn't bring on a hangover, lost wallets, overdrawn bank accounts, STD's, illegal sex, out of wedlock pregnancy, or spiritual condemnation.

When you begin to think on the things of God and want to do those things, then you are really ready to be married and enjoy the gifts and the **Fruits of Marriage.**

If you are already married and are still living in the world, you do the covenant and spouse a disservice, and you mock God. Get saved. (See **Rule 54;** *Fornication & Whoremonging.*)

Rule 29   Put On the New Man

Put On the New Man which looks like God and is also created in Righteousness (Eph 4:25). Get saved. Marriage is a gift from God for those **first** in the Covenant of Salvation. **Marriage will try, and it will work out your salvation** (Php 2:12). When you're ready to begin to look more like Christ, you're ready for marriage. You are created in God's image and likeness and crowned with Glory and Honor. Walk in it. **(Rule 17: *Righteousness*.)**

Rule 30   Put Away Lying

Put Away Lying; Speak Only Truth, (Prov 6:17; Eph 4:26 1Pe 2:1 and Col 3:9). Poor, or lack of communication is one of the main reasons for failed marriages. Couples MUST communicate truthfully with one another. One of my favorite people ever, said to me when asked a very hard question, *"Marlene, you will not like the answer to that question, and I'm never going to lie to you, so I'm not going to answer it."* To me, that was a perfect answer. I'd rather have no answer than a lie.

Everything you do affects everyone; even people you don't know. **Everything you do affects your spouse GREATLY.** When you lie (any sin), you open the door to the devil to come in and whip up on you, **and** your unsuspecting spouse. (And you say you *love* him/her?) Plus, you will be found out eventually, anyway. So, it would be better to come clean now. (See **Rules 12, 20, 30, 32, 35, and 102.**)

Prayer

If you are a liar or have lied, you need to repent **Father: In the name of Jesus I repent of lying, deceit, guile error, telling partial truths or falsehoods. I repent and revoke every lie told. Please forgive me, Lord, and cleanse me from all iniquity. Fill me with Truth.**

Satan, you are the father of lies; you are not my father, I live and breathe and have my salvation in the Lord Jesus Christ. I am a child of God. Satan, get out of my life and out of my heart and mind, I will only serve the Lord Jesus. I vow to speak the Truth in love from this day forward. In the Name of Jesus, Amen.

Rule 31   Lay Aside Malice

Lay Aside Malice (Meanness) (Eph 4:31, Col 3:8, 1Pe 2:1). Malice is related to sadism: the *desire to see someone suffer*. It is very demonic. If you choose to be married, desiring to see your mate prosper should be your goal, not seeing him or her suffer. Adult children of sadistic parents, who have not yet come to terms with their childhood, may bring

Malice into the marriage, unknowingly. They may not realize that Malice is in them and may think this is how you conduct a relationship. But, with Jesus, once you receive salvation and especially the Holy Spirit, allow Him to take away everything that is not like Jesus and then you can **tell the devil: Malice doesn't live here anymore.** (See **Rule 46.**)

Rule 32   Put Away Guile

Put Away Guile (Eph 4:31, 1 Peter 2:1; 3:10, Rev 14:5). Guile is *skillful deceit*. It is used by conmen, spies, and agents of the devil. Guile tells partial truths; it constructs scenarios to make things *appear* one way when they are actually another. Guile creates distractions to cover up the real deal – if you are full of Guile or Malice, you really need deliverance and much counseling (after salvation and a good dose of the Holy Spirit). **Control addicts** use Guile to manipulate situations and people to have their way. These two, Malice and Guile are not marriage-makers, they are **marriage-breakers.** Manipulation is a form of Guile and witchcraft (1 Sam 15:23). Stop the games! (See **Rule 150.**)

Prayer

Father: In the Name of Jesus, I repent of every work of the flesh. Forgive me of Lying, Malice, Guile. Remove the *spirits of lying, malice, guile* and *hypocrisy* from me.

Lying, Malice, Guile: I will not serve you anymore! Father, cleanse me with the Blood of Jesus. Fill me anew with Your Spirit, fill me with Truth, *Agape* Love, honesty, and sincerity that I may represent Christ in the Earth. Take away the sin, and the iniquity, in the Name of Jesus. Amen.

Rule 33   Put Away Hypocrisy

Put Away Hypocrisy (1 Tim 4:2; 1 Peter 2:1). Hypocrisy is lying about what you believe in, as in going along with the crowd, doing/saying what everyone else is. If you do not believe in marriage, do not get married. Do not act as if you do because others are, or peer pressure. If you don't believe in God don't marry someone who does. If you don't believe in worshipping in church with your mouth, tithes, and offerings, don't marry someone who does. If you do not believe in disciplining children, but your mate does, don't lie, then after you have the children, fight about it. God hates hypocrites; Jesus threatened the pretenders asking, **Why do you tempt me?** (Matt 22:18). (See Rule 119.) Be for real, come correct, tell the truth, be married for life and have a good time with your spouse.

Rule 34   Put Away Envy & Jealousy

Put Away Envy & Jealousy (Eph 4:31; Gal 5:21). People say that envy is a compliment; it isn't. It is bad feelings or discontentment about the qualities or *stuff* another has. Envious people are like miserable, lazy landscapers, always *looking* at green grass, but discontent with their own lawns. You can't enjoy your mate if you are envious, because of looking at others and their stuff. Get envy in check. If not, your spouse will feel inferior or rejected by your envious actions and attitudes, and you will probably have a lot of fights. If you are envious or jealous *of* **your mate** your have a real problem. Deliverance and counseling are indicated. If already married: Repent; seek deliverance, counseling. Ask the Lord for help.

Rule 35   Put Away Evil Talk

Put Away Evil Talk (Eph 4:31, Col 3:8-9). Out of the abundance of the heart, the mouth speaks (Mtt 12:34) If you think evil, you will talk evil. Further, a man can have whatever he says (Mk 11:23). You may have the evil you say, even if it is toward someone else! Cast down imaginations; that is, stop evil while it is only a thought and bring it under subjection to the Word. Your evil talk may bring evil to you or your family--, knock it off! If you want a successful, happy marriage, think on and talk on that--, not on evil. (See Rules: 32, 44; 46, 55, 59,96.)

Rule 36   Be Angry: Sin Not

If Angry; Sin Not, (Eph 4:25). Simple anger is an emotion; sustained, chronic, or uncontrolled anger is a *spirit*. Selfish anger is a response to not having your way. Grow up. Make no plans while angry, they will be evil plans--, always (Ephesians 4:26). Have emotions; but let the emotions go *through* you, not run your life. Be Spirit-led, not emotion-led. Godly, successful marriage are Christ-led and Word-led. (See **Rule 46**.)

Rule 37   Do Not Let the Sun Go Down

Let Not the Sun Go Down on Your Wrath (Eph 4:26; Col 3:8). Just formed or growing Wrath is bad, mut mature Wrath can lead to murder. Old Wrath is a terrible thing., it is the source of family feuds, generational curses, chronic unforgiveness, roots of bitterness, sickness, illness, death. Sin is the beginning of evil; when sin grows up it becomes death (James 1:15). How many days (suns) does it take for Wrath to grow up? I don't know. You don't know. Depends on what you feed it. Don't rehearse or think on it. Don't replay it over and over in your mind. Don't plan ANYTHING while angry. If engaged, disclose problems with anger. Seek the Truth; there's help! Submit to deliverance and counseling before you hurt yourself, marriage, or family.

Listen to one another. Work out Wrath before bedtime for your emotional and physical health! She may not be angry at you, you may not be angry at her, but either of you may need to work out the wrath you feel toward a *situation* that may have happened that day. Be there for each other! (**Rules 9, 46.**)

Rule 38   Tender Mercies

Tender Mercies (Lamentations 3:22-23, Col 3:12). Your spouse is due some Tender Mercies. If you're arguing, and cannot seem to finish the argument, check the clock. At 12:01 am, it's anew day and you're both due some Tender Mercies. Stop fighting!

Our God is full of Grace and Mercy, but what is a *Tender Mercy*? The Lord's Tender Mercy is because of His compassion for us, His ability to put Himself in our place to feel what we are going through and to respond out of *agape* love He has for us, His Mind of Christ and soul prosperity. So, you're yelling at your spouse, suddenly it's 12:01 am (by the clock, or it's 12:01 in the *Spirit*) you suddenly get a surge of compassion. You imagine how your mate must be feeling, being jumped on, yelled at, screamed at, unappreciated--, maybe deservedly so, but for some reason you just stop yelling. You just put yourself in your mate's shoes. (That was very Christlike.)

Jesus was also touched with the feelings of our infirmities (Hebrews 4:5). Tender Mercies.

Just as you want and need, you must give your mate some Tender Mercies. Do something new the next time you have an argument, give Tender Mercies.

(See also **Rule 48**, *Be Tenderhearted.*, **Rule 23,** *Access the Mind of Christ,* and **Rule 110,** *Prosper in Your Soul.*)

Rule 39   Give No Place to the Devil

Give No Place to the Devil (Eph 4:27). Evil thoughts, plans, intents, and actions give *place* to the devil; it invites him into the situation. When you're married, and you let the devil in, you're not just letting him into you --, you bring home a whole lot of negative spiritual stuff for your spouse to have to spiritually fight, succumb to, or fall under. How inconsiderate is that?

The devil and evil spirits inhabit dry places (Matthew 12:43). *Dry,* as a spiritual term means there is no water, no life, no Spirit of God. Dry places are waste and desolate places... those "places" could be *people* or *in a person.* Since the Spirit of God is supposed to dwell in people, when He is NOT there, the person is a **dry** place. When your place is dry, it's just as the devil likes it and he will come to *dwell.*

Have you ever read this on a label: Store in a cool, dry, or dark place? That's what the devil is looking for. Man's *cool* is not cool to God, who **says be hot or cold**. The Word says don't be lukewarm (Revelations 3:16). He doesn't say much about *cool,* but cool is just a few degrees below lukewarm.

Cool, dark, dry places is where the devil likes to live. And, where the devil is, is hell. But where the Spirit of the LORD is there is life, liberty, love, righteousness, peace, and joy in the Holy Ghost (Romans 14:17). Turn on the Light of Jesus, the Word, and *agape* love inside you and the devil will scatter like the roach that he is. *Put on the whole armor of light* (Romans 13:12).

Rule 40   Steal No More

Let Him Who Stole Steal No More (Ephesians 4:29). The old folks say, If you will lie, you'll steal, if you'll steal, you'll kill. We serve a God who is full of Grace and Mercy, and although He will not always strive with man (Genesis 6:3), He gives ample opportunity for repentance. If you were, or are a thief, anything from cheating on the time clock at work, to speeding on the highway – steal no more. Being married, everything you do affects your mate and home. What you do even now affects your children who may not even be born yet but are your *future*. Stop doing wrong, you know better anyway and do what is right in the eyes of the Lord. (See also, Shalt-*Not* VIII; Rule 11.

Rule 41   Get A Job

Labor; get a job, work with your hands, (Ephesians 42:8). A job can be your own business as well as ministry if the Lord says. If you're a man without a job, don't get married. Get the job first. Report regularly. Pay tithes, give offerings, save, and invest. No woman wants to marry an adult child who doesn't know how to do these simple things for himself. If you are a woman, you could do the same. The trend now is to work your job at home. A man who doesn't work should not eat (2 Thessalonians 3:10). Working a job is good discipline. It will keep you from stealing because you'll be busy working and you'll have money for the necessary things of life.

Rule 42   Have Abundance

Have abundance in your marriage, (Ephesians 4:28). Marriage is one of the delightful promises of the Lord, along with hundreds of others in the Bible. A married couple is an *entity* that can put 10,000 to flight and should never lack for money, houses, cars, food. Abundance should come to you because of who you are, whose you are, and that you are in covenant with God and one another. Abundance is promised to you. Work it as you become one and walk in Dominion.

You can have abundance all by yourself. Therefore, you should have 10 times more abundance *with* your marriage partner than as a single. One can put 1000 to flight, two, 10,000, (Deuteronomy 32:30). That's 10 times more power.

Riches & honor are with Wisdom, (Proverbs 3:8-19).

MARRIAGE ED, Rule 43

Share (Eph 4:28). generously, cheerfully. Couples: the husband and wife are prophetic visions. As the couple *becomes*, they look like Christ and His Church. Christ was generous, feeding multitudes more than once, healing all that came. The Church is the Earth's representative having light and answers for a lost and dying generation. We share the Good News of the Gospel, *and* sometimes folk need food or shelter. A married couple should *represent* and have extra to share generously and cheerfully. Hint: God does not like hoarders, (2 Corinthians 9:7.)

Rule 44   No Corrupt Communication

Let no corrupt communication proceed out of your mouth. (Ephesians 4:29, Colossians 3:8, 1 Peter 3:8-9). The Bible describes, *corrupt* as worthless or rotten. If what you say, especially to your mate, is not edifying or comforting, shut up. If arguing, don't assassinate your mate's character, criticize anything that cannot be changed. Be quiet. Your momma told you if you didn't have anything good to say, don't say anything at all. When you speak words that sow to the flesh, you will reap that, not your mate. Words that hurt or injure, especially if you are having fun doing it because of malice, will come back *on you*, not just wound the person you're directing it toward.

Your mate is expecting you to speak good things into his or her life, needing, maybe depending on it. After all, who else will? Who else knows your mate as you do? Who else will *agape* love him or her? Who else has **authority** to speak into his or her life? Hardly anyone. *Tag--*, you're it.

(See **Rules 35,59,65,96**.)

Rule 45   Grieve Not the Holy Spirit

Grieve Not the Holy Spirit. Grieve not the Helper, (Ephesians 4:30). I speak, especially of the wife, who is the *helpmate* in the marriage. Husband, do not grieve the *spirit* of the helper that is your wife. Let her help you. Self-reliance is a sin when you do it to God. Don't be so independent. It gets old and fosters rejection.

The wife doesn't get the Helper's anointing for marriage until the *I dos*. All other *help* you give is out of her flesh--, and it's exhausting.

Rule 46   Put That Away

Put that away. All works of the flesh. Bitterness (Ephesians 4:31) is tough to get rid of because it has a *root*. If you have ever tried to kill Crabgrass or Johnson grass, you know it takes some work to get the root out. Bitterness will come out with fervent prayer, fasting, deliverance, and strong resistance to it on your part. Ask the Holy Spirit to fill you and stick with the *spirit of forgiveness* and *agape* love. (Gal 5:19-21.)

Wrath

We've spoken about wrath in **Rule 37**. It is mentioned again in Ephesians 4:31. When something God mentions something more than once. It is very important.

Anger (See Rules 35, 36, 37, and 38.)

Clamor

Clamor is loud talking, protesting, sustained noise (Ephesians 4:31). Putting clamor away is God's way of saying shut up. Be quiet. The more junk you talk, the more likely it will be evil junk, and the more likely you are to make evil plans. Jesus could have said a lot of thing during His beatings, but He opened not His mouth, (Isaiah 53:7, and 8:32).

Evil Speaking (See Rules 35, 44, and 46.)

Malice (Ephesians 4:31, Colossians 3:8, Titus 3:3, 1 Peter 2:1c) (Rules 36, and 37.)

If God said it more than once. Pay attention.

Rule 47   Be Kind to One Another

Be kind one to another, (Ephesians 4:32, Colossians 3:12). It's a shame that God has to tell Christians to be kind to one another. It's even more of a shame when he has to tell married folk to be kind to one another. Do you think you could be consistently *kind* to your mate? Then get married; if not, don't. You mate is the perfect test of your *agape* love. Somebody who lives with you 24/7, who is that close to you--do you have *agape* for that person? You can't *agape* anyone until you are kind. Further *kind* is not all, but it's part of it. Nice or kind is not all there is to love, but it is foundational to it.

(See **Rule 17, Bear Fruit:** *Agape* **Love,** and **Rule 20.**)

Rule 48   Be Tenderhearted

Be tenderhearted, (Ephesians 4:32, Colossians 3:12). I like the term *tender hearted.* I used it to describe people who cry easily finding those people fascinating. Being tenderhearted toward God means you yield to him very easily in all things totally committed. Being tender hearted to your mate is what brings you those tender mercies discussed in **Rule 38**. A tender-hearted person is not hard hearted, stiff necked, rebellious, overly independent, insensitive, or uncaring but is easily moved to feel what another person is going through. It's akin to meekness, **Rule 17**. He or she is sympathetic and can easily pity his or her mate. Be merciful with balance be tenderhearted when speaking the truth in love, **Rule 20**.

Rule 49   Forgive One Another

Forgive one another, even as God for Christ's sake has forgiven you, (Ephesians 4:32, 1 Peter 3:8). Unforgiveness hurts you worse than the one you're not forgiving. It causes sickness, disease, in the grudge holder. It manifests neck problems and settles in the kidneys. Be resilient; it as a sign of soul Prosperity, **(Rule 110)**. If you can bounce back quickly, you are marriage material. If you or your mate cannot find *center* quickly from your own moods and feelings brought on by life's challenges and setbacks, you are in for head and heart aches. Get on your knees. Brace yourself, pray. If you're the one who can't come back to center quickly or you don't forgive readily, you could be guilty of taking the "f" out of fun. When *fun* becomes *un*, nobody is having any. When neither of you is fun, it's extremely difficult to *become one.* Deliverance and or counseling is indicated to find out why.

I used to brag about how long I could hold a grudge. Later I forgave but didn't forget. Neither grudge holding nor not forgetting is of God. Forgive your mate, and others, even as you are forgiven, then forget about it.

Recommended book: **Devil Weapons:** *Anger, Unforgiveness & Bitterness*, by this author.

Rule 50   No Payback
No payback, no retaliation. Do not render evil for evil. Instead, bless one another, (1 Peter 3:9).

Rule 51   Follow God
Follow God. As innocently as children and with purity of motive, Follow God, (Ephesians 5:1).

Rule 52   Walk in Agape Love
Walk in *agape* love, (John, 15:9-13, Ephesians 5:2, Colossians 3:14, 1 Peter 4:8). You won't walk in *agape* love without faith. (Ephesians 5:2 and you can't love until you find out what love is. Let's refer to the Love Chapter, (1 Corinthians 13).

LOVE IS:

Long-suffering, one suffers well, no matter how long, 13:4.

Love is kind, but it is more than just nice or kind, 13:4.

Love does not envy. Envy is a work of the flesh. *Agape* is spiritual. They don't mix, 13:4.

Love is not puffed up. It is not *prideful* (Proverbs 6:17).

Love behaves. It is not tacky, but it has decorum. 13:5.

Love doesn't only love what is good, too it 13:5.

Love is not easily provoked 13:5.

Love does not think on evil 13:5.

Love rejoices in truth, not in sin, or lies 13:6.

Love bears all things 13:7.

Love believes all things 13:7. Love has faith.

Love hopes all things 13:7. Faith is the substance of hope.

Love endures all things. 13:7 Love has faith.

Love never fails. 13:8 Love has promise and power with it.

LOVE IS NOT:

Love is not just being nice to folk.

Religion or going through the motions of religion.

Only giving things to the poor, doing good deeds.

Can you agape love? Anyone who?

_____

Are you willing to *agape*?

_____

Are you currently *agape*-ing anyone? Through what unlovely situation?

_____

In what ways are you willing to *agape love*?

_____

And what things do you need to walk more in *agape* now that you've seen the list on the preceding page?

Who's the hardest person or the most difficult situation, where you've had to *agape* someone?

Can your mate *agape*? Who?

_____

If you are not currently *agape*-loving your spouse. What thing or things does he or she need to **change** in order for you to begin to *agape* love him or her?

_____

Hint: *The last question above is a trick question. Agape-ing someone does not require them to change. You accept and love them as they are.*

` Make your beloved your best friend, (Song of Solomon, 5:16). Leaning emotionally on another, especially of the opposite gender, is emotional adultery. (See also Rules 10, 17,20. 47.)

Rule 53   Be Willing to Sacrifice

Be willing to sacrifice yourself as Christ did. (Ephesians 5:2). This rule mostly applies to men, as the man is to *become* the husband who treats his wife as Christ treats the Church.

Women to have a Christian walk, we all should be willing to give ourselves *for* one another not *to* one another. Do not give yourself away, that's slavery, except to be the bond servant of Christ. But what is in you that is for ministry to another, especially your mate, give that *for* him or her, (1 John 3:16).

Christ gave Himself as a sacrifice. Are you willing to make any sacrifices for your mate? OT husbands gave their wives offering sacrifices to give at church. Also, can you sacrifice to do something special for him or her? Stay up late? Get up early? Can you forgo getting the new car or other item to get something for your mate? That would really be memorable. I ask again, can you get up early or stay up late **to pray** for or with your mate?

Jesus' sacrifice was a sweet-smelling savor to God; Jesus was willing to be consumed in the process of the sacrifice. No one is asking you to be *consumed*, but can you smell good to your mate. Hint. Prayers and worship smell really good. And Christ gave his life for us because he first loved us, (John 10:15, 1 John 4:19) (See **Rule 68,** *Submit One to Another.*)

Rule 54   Fornication & Whoremongering
Put away fornication and *whoremongering,* (Ephesians 5:5, Colossians 3:5). The body is not for fornication, (1 Corinthians 613b).

Fornication is sexual contact with anyone *or thing* who is not your covenanted marriage partner. *Whoremongering* is chasing after anything, broadly that feeds a lust, especially sexual lust. Abstain from fleshly lusts which war against your soul, (Proverbs 6:32, 1 Peter 2:11). You need your **whole** soul to serve and worship God. When you tear off pieces of your soul, you diminish your capacity to serve God, put your spiritual destiny at risk, and embarrass God. Remember the Accuser of the

Brethren is in there accusing you anyway, (Zechariah 3:31). He seeks to damage the entire Body of Christ, humiliate, and hurt your spouse, soul tie yourself to a stranger, risk STD's sow *whoredoms* into your marriage and family--children, born and unborn, and a host of other things, as well as potentially pick up every demon that the person who fornicated with you has.

If you can't **contain**, marry, (1 Corinthians 7:9). That is, if you feel you *just have got to have it,* get married.

Premarital sex sows *whoredoms* into your marriage leading to distrust. *If he/she will do that to me with me in secret on the sly with whom else will they do it?*

Now that you're married, put that stuff down, *let your spouse satisfy you at all times,* (Proverbs 5:19, 7:5-27). (See Rules 25. 28 and 46.)

Rule 55   Put Away Uncleanness

Put away uncleanness, (Ephesians 5:3, Colossians 3:5). A child of God is to put away all uncleanness, which means is to not be morally defiled, foul, dirty or impure in actions, words, and appearance. Don't even give the appearance or hint of evil. (1 Thessalonians 5:22) don't play with the world. A meek and quiet spirit is of a great value to the Lord, (1 Peter 3:4). When you marry, decency is the very least of what is expected of you by your mate. OT: If a woman was deemed not to be a virgin on her wedding night, she could be divorced the very next day. Of course, if she was a virgin, she wasn't after that night.

Give no appearance or hint of evil. Purity pays. (See **Rules 28. 56. 57.**)

Rule 56   Get Rid of the Pornography

Get rid of the pornography (Proverbs 6:25-28). I don't care what you used to do or what you're used to looking at, you're saved now. Further, you are a married or engaged person now; get that filth out of your house and marriage, especially if you have children. Kids are smart and curious. There's nothing in your house that your children don't know or won't know about. They can find anything in the house except the match to their own socks. There's nothing worse to a child than having childhood innocence suddenly snatched away by pornographic images. Submit to cleansing by the Word and deliverance. Be rid all addictions--, pornography included. Pornography is demonically charged and is virtual adultery.

Rule 57 Put Away Filthiness

Put away filthiness, (Ephesians 5:4, Colossians 3:8). The Bible describes Filthiness as *obscenities*. If you have not put away the obscene thinking, language, materials, pornography, and filthy talk since you've been saved, by all means put it away from you when you take your salvation to the next level by getting married. Some people need to be delivered from profane talking such as the *spirit of cursing like a sailor.* (Also refer to Rules 28, 56, 57.) Ask the Lord to help; seek deliverance in your own church, along with counseling.

Rule 58 Put Away Idolatry

Put away covetousness and idolatry, (Ephesians 5:3-5, Colossians 3:5). Covetousness, and other things, leads to idolatry. God is saying over and again to put away the *old man*. He is laying it out clearly for your salvation. When you get married, which is another level of salvation, these same commandments apply. Appreciate what you have. Worship the Lord. Appreciate, honor, put value on your spouse and you won't be distracted by what someone else has. If you see a married person esteeming their mate, it may not be because their mate is so great. It is because that person knows how to treat their spouse well. *Duh!* Take a lesson: don't covet another spouse just because they look happy. (Idolatry is spiritual adultery.) Covet your own spouse. Covet the best gifts, (1 Corinthians 12:1). Isn't your mate the best gift you've ever gotten from God. (See Rule 13.)

Rule 59   Put Away Foolish Talking
Put away foolish talking and jesting, (Ephesians 5:4). You do know that you will have to give account of every word spoken while alive on Earth, don't you, (Matthew 12:36)? Speak words that build up, edify, comfort, admonish. Speak the words that the Lord gives you to say. Speak words of peace, not war. Speak words of increase, not decrease. Speak words that heal and don't hurt. Fun has its place, but when you get married, ungodly jesting has to stop. If not, who will know when to take you seriously? Will the ministering spirits of God, the angels, know when you were playing and when you were seriously praying? Don't risk it. Don't speak foolish words over or about your mate. He or she will really appreciate it. (See also James 3:10.) Use that breath and time to give thanks instead.

Don't embarrass your mate in public by saying things about him or her, acting the clown if it bothers your spouse or makes you look ignorant or stupid. *When I was a child, I spake as a child,* (1 Corinthians 3:11).

Vain jangling is babbling. Stop it (1 Timothy 1:6). (See Rules 35, 44, 65, 59, 94.)

Rule 60   Don't Be A Busybody

Don't be a busy body, (1 Peter 4:15). Don't gossip. Mind your own business and keep your marital business to yourself. I mentioned in my book, **_Behave_** that you need to keep your mind on your own life. Evil communications, corrupt good manners, (1 Corinthians 15:33). (See Rule 74.)

Rule 61   Give Thanks

Give thanks with a Grateful Heart, (Ephesians 5:4, Colossians 3:15b). Be truly thankful daily giving thanks to God draws you very close to Him. When you are appreciative and also give thanks to God for your mate, you are ready to be married. When you freely appreciate your mate openly and honestly, you are really ready to be married. You won't have to demand, trick, or coerce, which is witchcraft, a form of rebellion--, your mate into doing anything for or with you. Because of your thankful attitude and heart, your mate will gladly do many things for you and on your behalf. It will make your *becoming one* that much more assured. *Give thanks always for all things to God the Father in the name of Jesus Christ,* (Ephesians 5:20).

Three Things:

Name three things for which you are thankful to the Lord today.

_____

Name three different things for which you are eternally grateful.

_____

Name three things you will be thankful for tomorrow.

_____

Rule 62   Obey God

Obey God; do not be disobedient, (Acts 5:29, Ephesians 5:6). Your disobedience brings the ill-favor of God to yourself, your house and marriage. Even if *you* choose to suffer the wrath of God, your mate does not. Do not marry if you are going to bring judgment into your marriage. Obey all **MARRIAGE ED. Rules,** especially the Shalt *Nots*. **Rules 5 through 13.**

Disobedience, which is rebellion akin to witchcraft, brings on the Curse of the Law which is poverty, sin and eternal death. Is that what you want? Is that what you, your spouse wants?

If you are already married, repent and be wise, shunning evil. Choose right. Choose life!

Rule 63   Correct the Disobedient

Correct the disobedient, darkness and works of darkness, (Ephesians 5:11, Colossians 3:6). Tell the disobedient that what they're doing is wrong. If you get the opportunity. If not, have the good sense to shun their works. Shed light. for their sakes, (Ephesians 5:9). If you do not shun evil but joke about it, make fun of it--, if you appear to enjoy watching it, your mate will think that you're interested in it, or worse, doing it yourself. **Don't even talk about evil and works done in darkness.** Dirty jokes are unbecoming to godly marriage. *Evil communications, corrupt good manners* (1 Corinthians 15:33). Now that you are of the Light, shed light wherever you go. If you don't, you're disobedient. Because how can a light not *shine*?

Rules 64   Do Not Hang With Disobedient

Do not hang out with the disobedient, (Ephesians 5:11, 1 Peter 4:3-4). The Bible says don't run with them, even if you're doing it just for fun,

(Ephesians 5:6, 1 Peter 1:3,14,17). Again, *bad manners corrupt good morals.* Disobedience rubs off on you sooner or later. Baby disobedience shows up as laziness, procrastination, and stubbornness. When it is full grown, it is seen as and call full-fledged disobedience and rebellion.

If, saved, hanging out with the disobedient not to minister to, but to socialize with them, validates them, God can't correct or judge them because you're there. So, they don't learn anything. Or if God gets tired of your disobedience, since you know better, you will get judged with them!

Mates don't appreciate spouses habitually hanging out with bad boys or bad girls. When married, you are expected to choose good friends, not only single friends, but also married friends. If not, your mate may consider that suspicious behavior. Have like-minded couple friends, and covenant friends, not just associates. Allow God to choose your friends for you. Then you're ready for marriage. If you're married with shabby, raggedy friends that God, and spouse told you to get rid of years ago, do it. Obey God, honor your spouse.

Do I hang out with bad boys or girls?

_____

Why?

_____

What must I do to change that?

_____

Make your spouse your beloved and your best friend (SOS 5:16.)

Rule 65　Do Not Be Drunk

Do not be drunk with wine, (Ephesians 5:17). Alcohol and drugs quicken and make alive the flesh _temporarily_ just long enough to be tempted to sin, (1 Peter 3:18). A mate met in a bar is probably a drinker. Whether you're a drinker or not, being drunk causes the loss of self-control and guards are let down. That should not be. This will surely get you and your marriage in trouble. Drunkenness causes poor decisions and foolish acts. It is the mainstream of foolish talk, jesting, evil, corrupt communication which you should avoid. Drunkenness makes some people nice; some very mean. Others forget, but even if you don't remember or pretend not to remember what happened while you were under the influence, that doesn't let you off.

Drunkenness is dangerous if you operate heavy equipment, trucks, cars, motorcycles. But the real heavy machinery of your life is the vision of God, your marriage mission, and your spiritual purpose. Heavy machinery is your marriage, spouse, or any of God's people. They are fearfully and wonderfully made. Hands and mouth off any of this if drunk.

Receive deliverance from drunkenness and alcohol (for your Christian walk, representation, ministry, and marriage). *Watch, pray and be sober*, (Matthew 26:41, Mark 14:38, Luke 21:36, 1 Thessalonians 5:6). Drunkards do not inherit the Kingdom, (Galatians 5:21). You do expect to see your spouse in Heaven, don't you? If married, your spouse has to put up with this long enough. Get help.

Rule 66   Be Filled With the Spirit

Be filled with the Spirit, (Eph 5:18). One's flesh should be put to death, but be quickened in your spirit, (1 Peter 3:18b). Quickened means brought to life, made alive. By now you know that you can't obey the Ten Commandments without the Holy Spirit. You should have found out also that you cannot follow these **MARRIAGE ED.** Rules without Him, either. Especially you should have found out that *becoming* a husband or wife cannot be done without the Holy Spirit, who teaches guides, *quickens*, and leads you. The Holy Spirit also stirs up the anointing and the gifting in you to have the **ability** or power to *become* a husband or a wife. *Have you received the Holy Ghost since believing?* Acts 19:2

Rule 67 Speak in Psalms; Worship

Speak to your mate in Psalms, hymns, and spiritual songs, (Eph 5:19). Sing to your mate. Worship the Lord. Worship the Lord with your spouse. The Word is more powerful than a two-edged sword, (Heb 4:12), it is also edifying. The Word is what you were formed from and made of; it ministers to and grows you up. For best results, speak the Word to and over your mate, and he or she should speak it to and over you.

Rule 68 Submit to One Another

Submit to one another in love, (Ephesians 5:21, 1 Peter 5:6) **Husbands and wives sent me to each other as unto the Lord**. Yes, I said, *Submit to each other*! As the wife is submitted to the spiritual mission of the marriage, as does the husband and each member of the mission, marriage has an individual mission as well. Each mate is to help the other make fulfill his or her individual mission in the earth. The fulfilling of the marriage mission is the fulfilling of the individual missions should be complementary to one another. It is not **all** about the man or **all** about the woman.

Write the vision, make it plain, (Habakkuk 2:2).

Assignment: Write your marriage mission.

Rule 69   Remain Teachable

Remain teachable, (Proverbs 4:5-7, 8:33-35, 16:16). Both of you need an open, teachable spirit. Know-it-alls are no fun. Unteachable spirits are bores and chores. Husband, you have a helpmate, she might teach you a few things. Wife, your husband is wise in areas where you may lack. Learn from one another. God did not send you a mate who is as dumb as dirt with no spiritual qualities or values. Surely you allowed God to choose your mate for you? If you are teachable, you did.

How to remain teachable: Ask for a humble contrite spirit, which is excellent in God's eyes. Also, every night before bed I ask the Holy Spirit to teach me something.

Rule 70   Wife, Submit to Your Husband

Wife, submit to your husband as unto the Lord, (Ephesians 5:22, Colossians 3:1-6, 1 Peter 3:1). If you do not stay in submission, your prayers will be futile. A bunch of hot air going up into God's general direction. When you see a woman getting answers to prayers, you know she is in submission to her husband, whether he's in submission or not. When you see that man's prayers are answered, you know this because he is in submission to God.

Before marriage, **<u>MAKE SURE</u>** yours, your husband's, and God's definition of *submission* are all the same. It will save a lot of heartache. Learn the difference between *submission, subjection, subjugation,* (and repression, which is ***acting*** as though you're submitting to the mission of the marriage.)

Rule 71   Husband, Love Your Wife

Husband, Love your wife unconditionally as Christ loves the church. No matter how bad the wife is, what, she does or doesn't, hasn't done, give *agape* love without bitterness, (Ephesians 5:25, Colossians 3:19). Love her as Hosea loved in spite of Gomer's *whoredoms*. No matter what the mate does, you have to forgive 70 times 7, (Matthew 18:22). Rejoice, if your mate repeatedly makes the **same**

mistake. Hey, that's only **ONE** problem. And no problem is too big for God. Have you prayed diligently, fervently, without ceasing? Bound, loosed, (Matthew 18:18)? Have you *fasted* for the mate's breakthrough, (Mark 9:29). This is your beloved and your best friend, (Song of Solomon 5:16). You're in a *spiritual* union. Spiritual work is expected of you.

Rule 72   Husband: Maintain Headship

Husband: Maintain headship in the marriage, (Ephesians 5: 23-24). The Kingdom of God and authority work by headship. When there is no head, the Lord doesn't have the *point of contact* for the accountability that is required. God always appointed a head and names the husband, the man as the head over the wife, even as Christ, is head of the Church and God is the head of Christ, (Ephesians 5:23). Spiritual order is critical for God to flow in your marriage. Husband, maintain headship. Wife, submit (Ephesians 5:22). When perversion of the marital order presents, problems come into the marriage.

God especially hates sexual perversion. One of the main reasons being there is no head. There must be a man and a woman for God to recognize the union and marriage.

Stay in Authority; don't give it to your Wife unless you won't be home. Don't give it to your kids; your wife is second in command. Don't give it to your neighbor; don't seat your neighbor at the head of your dinner table. Maintain your position. God and Family will really appreciate that.

Rule 73   Husband, Give *For* Your Wife

Husband, give yourselves *for* your wife, (Ephesians 5:25). I didn't say give yourself *to* your wife. You are still your own person. But give all that the Lord is giving you four your wife to your wife. The Lord will restore you and make sure you do not run out of anything, (see Rule 53), be willing to sacrifice.

Rule 74   Husband, Sanctify Your Wife

Husband, sanctify and cleanse your wife with the washing of water by the Word, (Ephesians 5:26). Women will talk. Husband, if you don't give your wife something to carry, she may find something on her own or make up something. It's called gossip. Every time you speak the Word over your wife, she grows up a little more in the Lord because she is made of the Word, and words. She becomes more in love with you, more respectful of you, she honors you more and will submit all the more to the marriage. Trust me. You want that.

Use the Word of God as it was intended as a weapon to defeat the enemies of your marriage and as a tool to build it up, (Ephesians 5:26). (See also Rules 60).

Rule 75   Husband, Present Your Wife

Husband, present your wife to God, holy without spot, blemish, wrinkle, or any such thing, (Ephesians 5:27). Prepare yourself for this challenge. If you're not yet married, mighty Man of Valor, God is expecting that you will take excellent care of that Daughter of Zion and entrust her and it (the marriage) to your stewardship.

If you are already married, take a snapshot, (physical and spiritual) of your wife now and compare it to when you first married her to see if you are keeping your end of the stewardship deal. She should be **better** in every way now compared to how she was when you met her, (Eph 5:26). *Is she?*

Rule 76   Husband, Love Your Wife

Husband, love your wife as yourself, (Ephesians 5:28).

If you do not love yourself in a balanced way, not thinking more of yourself than you ought to, but hating yourself, you are not ready to be married. Allow Jesus to do a work in you first. If you don't, you will drive your mate nuts with your ups and downs. It's not fair unless you inform him or her in advance, and he or she agrees to go through your personal spiritual *process* that you are submitting wholeheartedly to God about, (Ephesians 5:28).

If you don't yet love yourself, it will be impossible to love anyone else. Still, the Bible makes it very personal for men, saying, **you,** in particular--, love your wife. Wife, see that you honor your husband.

Rule 77   Wife, Reverence Your Husband

Wife, reverence, honor and respect your husband, (Ephesians 5:33). What's not to love? Husband is using the Word in the house and at church. He's praying for and with you. He's giving himself *for* you. He's forsaking all others, leaving, and cleaving. He is respecting, loving, and honoring you first, just as Christ did the Church. This is easy. Any wife can submit to that.

But what if he's not? Then you've got to do your part anyway. When there was darkness, God sowed light. When there's nothing to love, honor and respect, do your part anyway then watch the Lord grow it.

Rule 78   Dwell According to Knowledge

Husbands dwell with your wife according to knowledge, giving honor that your prayers be not hindered, (1 Peter 3:7). Husband, take time to learn your mate. Learn what the Good Book says about women, and hear what God says about *your mate,* in particular. This takes time in prayer, the Word, and in the presence of God, alone and with your mate. Your wife is **not** a woman-at-large, she is special, unique, and marvelous in the eyes of God. If she is not also marvelous in your eyes, find out what makes her so special to God.

If the *"getting to know you"* process has ended, it could be because of premature, illegal sex. If you haven't made that mistake, don't make it. Sex is an *I don't* want to wait until **the** *I do's* are said in front of the preacher. Getting to know each other, learning one another may have stopped because of selfishness: *I got what I want. I don't have to do anything else. Or, I figured out how to open the milk carton, now I can have milk whenever I want.*

If you really want to know someone, leave sex out of the equation until marriage. Men: Make her your beloved and your best friend. If you have already opened the *carton* before marriage. Repent to God and to one another. Ask the Lord to restore purity, honor, and trust in your relationship.

Rule 79   Meet the Parents

Meet the Parents! *The fruit doesn't fall far from the tree, and neither do the nuts.* Meet **all** parents on both sides of the family Sit and talk with them. Get to know them. Who are they? What do they talk about? Look at them. How do they look? What is on their minds? Do they have memory? Do they only talk about the past? Positive or negative current events? Do they talk willingly about their lives, or do they seem close-mouthed? Ashamed? Do they teach and share? Do they control or manipulate your mate? Is he or she a different person when with the parents versus when the other people as compared to when along with you? Keep your eyes and ears open.

Have the parents aged well? Does the family live long (Ephesian 6:3), or are there early deaths? See how they age, sickly, quickly, or well? What is the spiritual application? Saved? Tithers? *For better or for worse, the fruit doesn't look too different than the tree.*

Introduce **all** your parents (and grands) to your intended as well, so he or she can know **you**.

Woman, your mate must know that you have a father, father figure or covering, this is critical for the respect you must receive. When someone thinks you have no father you are treated differently than if you did. Also, what are the things about your parents that you need to be diligent NOT to repeat?

Rule 80   Meet the Siblings

Meet the siblings. Meet every one that your intended spouse grew up with. Anyone that he or she talks about that made an impact on his/her life, good or bad, especially the brothers and sisters. Find out what their relationships were and are now. Especially note how a male treats his mother and sisters and how a female gets along with her dad and brothers Are their relationships normal and close? Are they *too* close? Have the children found that they are *separate* people yet or are they still the **unit** that their parents may have mistakenly raised them to be? It can be hard for many to separate and *individuate* if parents have grouped them together in one unit. Individuation should happen around age 2. My three younger sisters were all called by one name. Each was called by her own name, but they also were called together in rapid succession as if they were one person, and they usually did everything together, so they were most often together. They are each two years apart in age but used to being dressed **identically** until they were eight or nine years old.

They grew up anyway. When the oldest left home, it affected the middle child was not as much as the youngest was affected when the middle sister left home to be married. The youngest sister was a mess for more than 10 years, I believe that she had not had the opportunity to become herself. I saw this in my adolescence, regarding their collective childhood, and shared what I saw.

I was told that I was jealous, and to mind my own business. I knew that each needed to *become* her own person. As the trio split, my youngest sister felt abandoned, rejected; decades later, she is just now getting over it. My baby sister is single, but with those issues, what a horrible spouse she would have been.

If the other children had not become themselves individually, they could have been pulled back into the childhood dynamic as well. Do you see how all this could have attacked any marital *cleaving*?

Siblings can form Pain Cliques, or soul ties, (See Rule 17) and resist breaking apart even after they marry spouses and move away from one another. Some adult siblings don't or can't move away from each other.

Have I left home? _____

Physically *and* emotionally?

_____.

You can't stay home physically because you should get too big for your bunk bed. You can't stay home spiritually because God says you have to grow up and get a life. You can't stay home emotionally because too many adults in the same house is a disaster. You can't stay home naturally because the economic system is such that it is taking more and more to live on. Years have gone by and you need to get a job because your parents can't afford to take care of you anymore.

Have I become my own person in the Lord, or do I still need my siblings and childhood friends to validate me? _____

Am I in God's will for my life or are there a collection of people voting on what I should do or should be doing and directing me thusly?

_____

If married, have I cleaved?

_____

Rule 81   Meet the Relatives
Meet the relatives, <u>all</u> of them.

I have five uncles, three of them far past retirement age, never married. Of those three, two are in their 90s. My dear dad has a bond with his brothers that I've always considered excessive. I don't know if he had a *cleaving* problem, but I do know that his dad, who died before I was born, bonded the brothers together as boys so much that a few of them didn't seem to separate or *individuate* into individual people. Two of the three who never married never left home. I wondered if anyone including my mother ever came before my father's brothers in my father's mind or heart. The other married uncles seemed to cleave well to their mates, raise successful families, but I believe that their "family loyalty" was questioned by the other brothers who called them *henpecked*.

Because I recognize this, I don't judge or condemn my uncles, but after hearing the Word, the Truth, I make necessary changes for my own life. I choose to bond and cleave to my spouse without being too clingy to my birth and childhood family, as I'm no longer a child, (1 Corinthians 13:11).

A man should *leave his mother and father and cleave to his wife, and that the two should be one flesh*, (Ephesians 5:31). That also means that the man and woman now start a new family and will raise children to be adults who will do the same. Abraham, too had to leave the land of his birth in order to fulfill the will of God and reach his destiny.

Rule 82   Meet the Friends

Meet the friends. Friends are a very good source of information. What they do and *don't* say is valuable. What kind of folk they are speaks to what kind of folk your mate is, what he or she can tolerate or even enjoys? Pay attention.

What does your intended make do with his or her friends?

Is there high school behavior when around the friends?

Do they sneak off someplace to do their friendship thing out of your sight?

Are hours and hours at the mall or the gym involved in, they're hanging out.

Do they go out of town and leave you home?

Are the friends saved?

Are they married? Do they have children? How are they with or to their children/wife/families?

Are they serious or childish?

Do they have purpose and know it?

Or are they wandering in life?

Do you like film?

Do they like you?

Could you welcome or would you have tolerated any of them in your house? For how long?

How many of these friends are previous boyfriends or girlfriends to your mate?

How does that make you feel? Can you handle it?

How's your intended around his or her friends? About the same different silly serious.

Are these friends moochers or supportive?

Does your mate's friends have jobs?

Is your mate the leader of the friendship?

Is he or she the primary? Do these friends call your mate? If your mate doesn't call them or is it 1 sided? Proverbs 1824.

Is your major follower doing whatever the leader says.

Do you want these friends around your children when you have kids?

Do you want their kids around your kids?

Consider these things now. Don't wait until marriage and kids have to fight about it.

If you're already married, you should have mutually, ideally couple friends. Husband should have straight, sober, family-minded male friends and wives should have straight, sober, family-minded female friends. If your friends are from the same couple, they would be great. Pray together, ask the Lord to identify your covenant friends, associates, partners to you individually and as a couple.

Your spouse should be your friend on Earth. But if Jesus is not yet a friend of your intended, wait for marriage, but make the introduction. Jesus says, **You are my friends**, (John 15:14). In life you will need a friend like Jesus whether you're married or not.

Rule 83   Meet the Coworkers

Meet the coworkers. Go to his or her job. Meet the coworkers. They will spend almost as much or more time with your spouse as you do. The coworkers may have seen him or her in many more moods or situations than you have. At work your spouse is probably well known. Some coworkers, maybe friends. Some are like family. Meet them.

Is your mate comfortable on his or her job? Competent. Does he or she enjoy their life's work, or will he or she change up on you as soon as you marry? Will there be a sudden retirement? Will your spouse just quit their job? Will there be a financial surprise in your household after you marry? Meet the coworkers and the boss, if possible.

Is there stability?

Rule 84 Meet the Church Members

Meet the church members Anyone who is really involved in church spends a great deal of time and energy there. When you get to know the church members, including the pastor, you will learn a lot more about your mate.

Eventually, the decision must be made of which church will you join after marriage--, his or hers? None? Will just one of you go to church to **represent** the whole family? Will one of you renege on your dating *spirituality*? --you know, when you your dates were at church, or church was your *whole* date because that's where you met.

Speaking of **Dating Discipline**: How is your mate in church with you? Does he or she pray? Does he or she know where the Books of the Bible are when the pastor calls them out, does he or she worship? Does he or she tithe or give offerings? Does he or she go to discipleship training, Sunday school, or Bible Study during the week? Are you still dating?

If married, compare how it used to be when dating. Has your mate dropped the **Dating Church Discipline** or has your mate gotten better since you've been married? **Pay attention, this is an open book test. What you see is what you will get when you marry this individual.**

Rule 85 Obey Father & Mother

Children obey father and mother. Parents (Husband and Wife) see that your children obey you, (Ephesians 6:1, Colossians 3:20, Proverbs 6:20-29). Until you have the guts to discipline your children, don't have any, you'll ruin them, which is far worse than spoiling them.

When your children disobey you, they bring the Curse of the Law on themselves and into your house while they live with you. Sometimes that iniquity lasts longer than just while they are at home. Many parents are running to jails and courtrooms to rescue their children, (some of which are adults) who were always *such good children*. Parents, did you see your children as they really were, or only as you wanted them to be? As a married couple, it is your responsibility to raise your children the way God said, while not provoking them to anger, (Ephesians 6:4c, Rule 62. Rule 15). Do you remember this from **Rule 15**? If you didn't fill it out before, do it now.

Office title: Child

_____

Authority

_____

Rights

_____

Privileges

_____

What are the child's responsibilities and to whom is he responsible?

_____

To whom is the child accountable?

_____

Also see **Rule 8**

_____

Rule 86   Put On the Whole Armor

Put on the whole armor of God and be strong in the Lord and the power of his might (Ephesians 6:11). If you're not ready to defend your spouse, your marriage, and your home with prayer, fervent prayer, and spiritual warfare, don't get married.

If you're already married and not entering into spiritual warfare, no wonder your marriage is as it is.

Jesus said *the gates of Hell shall not prevail against the Church,* (Matthew 16:18). Don't you remember that the husband and wife are the model of Jesus and the Church? The Gates of Hell shall not prevail against you. If hell is wearing you out but you're not doing anything about it, you are disobedient. Further, (Matthew 18:18) says that *binding* and *loosing* is why and how the gates of Hell shall not prevail. Then Matthew says in 18:19 that if two agree as touching, excuse me, married couples: Are you praying? Are you *binding* and *loosing*? Are you agreeing? And since this is what you have to do the Lord also. by His Spirit, provided a full armor for battle.

Are you sure you're ready to be married? If you are, glory to God. Remember, you fight for and stand with your spouse, **never** *against* your spouse.

Your marriage partner is not your enemy, adversary or sparring partner.

Rule 87   Stand Against the Devil

Stand against the wiles of the devil, (Ephesians 6:10-11.) Wiles are tricks, strategies, seductions, devices, or procedures. The devil has a manual. I don't know if it's written down or not, but the devil seems to know things that will distract men. Once *distraction* is turned on, man pretty much does the rest of the stuff to himself, *himself*. The devil is limited in what he can do to man, but distraction is fair game. There are other tactics that he uses. Do you know what they are? How will you stand against him? How will you stand for your family? Learn the enemy's tactics so you can be married securely and successfully.

Rule 88   Stand Therefore

Stand therefore, (Ephesians 6:10-11, Ecclesiastes 4:10-12). One morning the Holy Spirit had me to get up and stand on my bed, so I did. *Foolish things confound the wise*, (1 Corinthians 1:27). I stood there right in the middle of the bed. After only a few seconds of standing there, I asked the Lord what was I standing there for?

He answered, **You are standing, therefore.**

Touché. I get it. No matter what *I feel* like what it *looks* like. I obey. I **stand, therefore**. He was teaching me to understand some of the tactics **we** have for warfare against the enemy.

Are you willing to stand there wherever *there* is **for** your marriage? Then you're ready for marriage.

Rule 89   Put On Truth

Gird your loins with truth, (Ephesians 6:14). Loins in the New Testament means your hip area is the area of your reproductive organs. Jesus is the Truth. The Word is Truth. If you are all wrapped up in the Truth, you will only reproduce what you are wrapped up in. If you're having a battle in your life, you need the Truth because it will make you free, (John 8:32).

The translation of that passage is *the truth shall free you free.* (And that's free indeed.) So, if you're in a battle and need to be freed, you need the Truth or the Word to do the work for you. Further, the more Word and Truth you have, the better. If you are reproducing Truth and the Word in the Earth, you have more defense and offense for victory than if you do not. Married and want-to-be-marrieds: Are you ready for this?

Fact versus the Truth. A fact is what it is. Truth is what God says. Speak what God says, in love. Don't just repeat what you see. **(Rule 20:** *Speak the Truth in Love,* **Rule 12:** *Shalt Not IX,*

Rule 30: *Put Away Lying,* and Rule 86: *Put On the Helmet.*)

Rule 90   Put On Your Shoes

Put on your shoes. Have your feet shod with peace, (Ephesians 6:15). Shoes on means you are ready for warfare. Shoes off means you're docile, homebound, retiring. Pregnant? It means no warfare. Shoes on means you can redeem, shoes off means you're not worthy to redeem anyone. John the Baptist knew that Jesus was the Redeemer but didn't feel worthy to unlatch the Perfect Man's shoes, (Acts 13:25). The Gospel of Peace is the Gospel of Jesus. Once again, the Word is *on* you. This time it's on your feet. Carry **The Message** and enjoy the peace of God, which is prosperity.

Husbands and Wives bring Peace in the house with you at the end of the day. Speak Peace over your mate, and home, and marriage daily. Again, be prepared to use the Word in any type of warfare and spiritual agreement and to resolve disagreements between you. Jesus is our peace.

Rule 91   Take the Shield of Faith

Take the shield of faith to quench the fiery darts of the enemy, (Ephesians 6:16). Faith believes what God says about you and your situations. Fiery darts try to pierce your faith, but since you have a shield, since you have faith, it is impossible to do. Instead, the darts will fizzle out. Fiery darts are things like negative words, thoughts, and situations that may arise that are contrary to what you will believe in God. Fiery darts hit you in your heart and gut as uncertainty, unbelief and doubt. Rise up in your faith and put the fiery darts out for yourself, and your marriage.

Rule 92   Put On the Helmet of Salvation

Put on the helmet of salvation, (Ephesians 6:18, 1 Thessalonians 5:8). Think saved thoughts. The helmet is the item of armor most intimate with the head. When you know what the end is, just as God said, it will be thoughts of peace and not of evil plans to give you an expected end, (Jeremiah 29:11). You will not let counter thoughts such as enemy warfare enter your head. Think good things about your mate, marriage, and future. Think on these things: *things that are lovely, pure, true have virtue, and are of good report,* (Philippians 4:8).

Rule 93   Take the Sword of the Spirit

Take the sword of the Spirit, (Ephesians 6:17). Only those experienced with the word or planning to be experienced with the Word should marry. The Word of God is quick, powerful, and sharper than any two-edged sword, (Hebrews 4:12). It should not be handled by children and novices. It can be very powerful and dangerous if not used properly.

When you know how to handle the sword *for* your spouse, not **against** your spouse, you're ready for marriage. Your marriage partner is not your enemy.

Rule 94   Pray Always

Pray always with all prayer and supplication, (Ephesians 6:18, Colossians 4:2a). Pray always is the first part of this **Rule**. Pray without ceasing, (1 Thessalonians 5.) That means your spirit man is prayerful, even when your lips aren't even moving. Prayer is not just for women. Are you married? Do you wanna be married? Then pray.

Pray all kinds of prayers. Don't just petition God all the time asking for things. There are more than a dozen types of prayer. You don't have to mix them all into every prayer that you pray, but there are occasions to use each kind, and sometimes you may pray more than one type with another.

Praying with supplication means to pray earnestly, fervently, humbly and many times with tears. Jesus did. Can you humble yourself before the Lord in prayer? Then you are ready to be married.

If you have no prayer life, your life will reflect that. Don't bring your prayerless drama to anyone, please.

Rule 95   Pray In the Spirit

Pray in the Spirit, (Ephesians 6:18). Stir up the gift when you pray in the Spirit, you speak directly to God. This is powerful for your marriage. If you can't ask God to give you the Holy Spirit with evidence of speaking in other tongues, or ask someone to minister the Holy Spirit to, you, (Acts 2:4, Jude 1:20).

Rule 96   Watch With Perseverance

Watch with perseverance, (Ephesians 6:18, Colossians 4:2b, 1 Peter 4:7, 5:8, 1 Thessalonians 5:6). Watching is so important that God established special people to do it, Watchmen. Ezekiel was a watchman, (Ezekiel 3:17). You may not have the anointing to be a watchman, but if God has told you to watch, there is anointing that is available to you to do just that, and then do something about it. Ask for it.

Jesus was upset with the people when He said that they knew the weather but could not discern the spiritual times, (Matthew 16:3). He implied that naturally they knew what was going to happen, but they didn't seem to care about the spiritual climate. Since the people of Jesus' time were agrarian and fishermen, they cared about the weather because it would affect their money but didn't look deeper into things of God. What's new?

Watch. You can watch when the Holy Spirit shows you something. It is usually so you will see it, learn from it, and then pray to correct it.

Watch for your family. Notice little things about your mate and children, if you have any, don't be critical. Know your spouse so that you can begin to pray immediately if things aren't as they should be.

Watch and be sober. **See Rule 65**. Do not be drunk.

Rule 97   Intercede for Your Mate

Intercede for your mate, (Romans 8:26-27, Hebrews 7:25). And also, fast. If you don't, now you have no intentions of praying for a spouse, don't marry. Don't marry someone who expects or needs you to pray for him or her. If you make the better or worse sickness or in health, richer and poorer, vow about 1/2 of the time, you're probably going to be needing to be praying. Sometimes people don't know how to, or they are too rebellious, stubborn, or lazy to pray for themselves. If that's your mate, you have the responsibility to pray for him or her first. Pray against ignorance, rebellion, stubbornness, and laziness.

Ideally, you should have begun praying for your mate when you first knew that you wanted to marry and knew how to pray. You should have, once you found out who you are in the Lord, and that your purpose is, begun to pray for your mate, married or not. Pray for a Godly mate whose purpose you are part of and vice versa. Pray the Word.

Godly parents began interceding or praying for your life's mate when you were born. Oh, so few are so blessed. But it's a new day. Are you praying for the mates of your children, born or unborn? Have you begun praying for your *children's* children? It's not too early and a good man leaves an inheritance to his *children's* children, (Proverbs 13:22)

Prayers transcend space and time. They are good inheritance. When the mate is going through, getting on your nerves, intercede. Pray in the Spirit. No soulish prayers.

Rule 98   Pray *With* Your Mate

Pray *with* your mate. If you have no intention of praying *with* your mate, don't marry anyone. If you are a prayerless mate, stay single. If you are a mate-less prayer, God may change your status. If married, God expects you to *become* one and one of the main ways you *become* one is in the prayer closet. When you develop spiritual intimacy, you get to know the real person and you develop a closeness that cannot be explained. Pray with others but pray with your own mate first and foremost.

If married, learn a new trick. Pray with your mate at least once a week, even if it's just an extended version of asking the blessing over your meal. After that, escalate to a short bedtime prayer As you part for work in the mornings, if you can't do that, join together and bless your children as they go off to school. Pray Psalm 23 or the blessing in Numbers 6:24-26: *The Lord bless thee and keep thee. The Lord make his face shine upon thee and be gracious unto thee. The Lord lift up his countenance upon thee and give thee peace.*

Now this is where the rubber meets the road. The two of you are expected to pray together for your children and your *children's* children. If you've never learned to pray together, how when do you think you'll suddenly start paying for your kids and grandkids? Get on with the business of becoming one and pray together. Intercede for others with your mate.

Rule 99   Be Bold

Boldness & Teaching: Open your mouth with boldness and teach the mysteries of God to one another (Ephesians 6:19-20). This Rule implies several things.

1. You know something about the mysteries of God and the Word of God.

2. The Heaven over you is open to revelation.

3. You are assured enough, (fully persuaded) to open your mouth and share what you know, believe and heard from the Lord.

4 You have relationship with God.

5. You are not ashamed of the Gospel of Jesus Christ.

6. When you're not doing the sharing but listening, you're the student; you're teachable.

Without revelation, you'll be boring, uninteresting--, dull like people who tell the same stories over and again--. Oh, for the Mind of Christ! Without God's *quickening*, you'll be uninteresting to your mate. Stale. You won't even realize how dull you are. Without the Spirit of God, you may be timid, unsure. But with God every day will be fresh, new, and exciting. The *quickening* of your spirit by God's Spirit brings life to your marriage.

Meet Him, *learn* Him, know Him, spend time with Him so that your time with your mate will be exciting and adventurous.

Rule 100   Have Peace & Joy

Have peace and joy, (Isaiah 55:12, John 15:9-11, Romans 14:17, 15:13, and Galatians 5:22). Do not marry if you do not have at least Peace, but ideally also Joy as your baseline when you could easily return to that *center* of Peace and Joy by yourself. Your mate is not responsible for your mood, you are. That you profess Christ as a plus, not so much that you'll go to Heaven later and to church now, but that you will:

- Speak the same language in your marriage.
- Be pleasant, decent to be around, and have a center or baseline of normalcy.

If you are a grouch, grump, or generally an unhappy person, marrying anyone will be out of your own selfishness. No one is interested in Oscar the Grouch on a daily basis. Especially in the mornings, I personally look forward to mornings--, tender *mercies,* anew day the Lord's favor. I awaken with the Lord on my mind.

Have Peace and Joy be a *lively* stone. The marriage cannot be built with dead weight, (1 Peter 2:4-5). Especially with second plus marriages and blended families, I recommend premarital counseling for at least six months and full deliverance for both parties, and their children if there are any. And if you can get the Ex's and the children, other parents in there, your parents and sibs--, DO IT! If you're prone to any wilderness attitudes or behavior, murmuring, complaining, etc., don't marry anyone until after deliverance and or deep, Christian counseling.

(Recommended: *The Wilderness Romance*, by this author, a 3 book series, *The Social Wilderness, The Sexual Wilderness* & *The Spiritual Wilderness*.)

Rule 101 Be Debt Free

Be debt free. Owe no, man, anything, (Romans 13:8).

If you have debt, no one wants to marry you. Why? It takes an anointing and deliverance to be made free of debt. That's why Jesus died so we could live because without deliverance your mate may also have debt and be planning on you helping him or her out of their debt. Without deliverance, folk continue in debt of all kinds.

Types of Debt

Financial - Your spouse pays $800 per month child support for the next 16 years. Not only is that financial debt, it is **emotional debt** because it's not being paid to the child, but the former spouse or the child's other parent. *Where your treasure is that's where your heart will be,* (Matthew 6:21). And it's spiritual. In my book, *Among Some Thieves,* I write about the effects of paying money on you and your *soul.* Yet with child support, alimony and other court ordered payments, you have no choice. Obey civil law.

We serve a debt-canceling God, a Redeemer. We have not the power to redeem ourselves or our children, (Neh 5:5).

Spiritual Debt. You aren't getting out of spiritual debt until you let the Redeemer save you.

Emotional Debt- Anything from still beating yourself up from having soul ties. Soul ties are emotional debts. Soul ties are full of works of the flesh and relate to the soul, especially the emotions. Hatred, unforgiveness bitterness and alike. Soul ties are intensely passionate. They do not always involve hate. Many times, there's love or the perception of love involved obsession.

People can be soul tied to their parents, siblings, children, whether or not there's custody battle and especially if there is. Losses, deaths and breakups that one just cannot seem to get over is evidence of a soul tie.

Physical Debt- If a person is paying a criminal debt with his or her physical body in jail or prison, they are not available for marriage in the traditional sense.

Time Debt- One source of time debt is the nine to five when you owe time to other people, even if it is an exchange for money. You're still in debt. Jesus' Disciples did not have any time debts. They were able to end, chose to stop what they were doing, to follow Him when He called.

Rule 102 Refrain From Evil & Guile

Refrain your tongue from evil. Speak no guile. Silence is a form of spiritual warfare, (See also Rules 32 and 35: *Put Away Guile and Put Away Evil Talk*.)

For he that will love life and see good days. Let him refrain his tongue from evil and his lips that they speak no guile. 1 Peter 3:10

You can't expect to speak blessings over your family if you also speak evil and guile. You cannot turn God on and off like a water spigot, (James 3:10). If married and not speaking, blessings over your spouse, begin today. Ask God to help.

Rule 103 Suffer Well

Suffer well. It is better to suffer for well doing than evil doing, (1 Peter 3:17). Yet it is more Christ like to suffer well than to suffer poorly. Suffering well is related to the Fruit of Longsuffering. Do not seek out suffering as those with a martyr complex, but if you have to suffer, suffer well. There's reward and anointing that follows Longsuffering. Afterward, God perfects establishes, strengthens, and settles you, (1 Peter 5:10b). After going through in marriage, the Word will perfect, mature, establish, strengthen and settle your marriage. (See **Rule 17**, *Bear the Fruit of the Spirit: Longsuffering*).

Rule 104   Do Not Be Unequally Yoked

Do not be unequally yoked, (2 Corinthians 6:14). Marriage is a spiritual bond between two spiritual people for the sake of creating righteous seeds. This cannot exist if one is *quickened* and then the other is dead in trespasses and sins. A suitable marriage partner is the in the same "grade" as you. In grade school, you would never "like" anyone who was in the grade below, not to mention two or three grades below. If you've been saved for ten years and the one you "like" just got saved last week, you're robbing the *spiritual* cradle. Don't do it. It's an unequal yoke. Yes, the Lord can redeem the time, (Ephesians 5:16), but let Him do His work first. Let the baby Christian apply himself to knowledge, Wisdom, and instruction (Proverbs 2:2) before marriage. You want to confuse your children? This will do it. One holy parent and one heathen. No unequal yokes!

Rule 105   Fight For Your Marriage

Be prepared to fight for your marriage, (1 Peter 4:12, 3:13). Humans don't seem to have gotten the revelation of marriage yet; they haven't acknowledged that marriage is a valuable, precious thing, and that is something that you must fight for and that it is worth fighting for. For that reason, too many seem too willing to throw it away or discard it.

Not everyone has a marriage. Not everyone who looks as though they have a marriage has a marriage. Some marriage partners are merely *associated* with one another. Some have a business arrangement of sorts, others mindlessly coexistent of habit. There is one form of marriage, and only one model. Christ and the Church.

The average marriage reflects any individual's relationship with God. Again, if you're ready to test your salvation or take it up a notch, get married. How people treat their mate is how he or she is treating God and how they believe God is treating him or her. Sad, isn't it? Sad when it should be, could be joyous.

Even within the same marriage, you can see two people who are having two completely different relationships with the Lord. One is having a love affair with God and the other is at war with Him. Go figure. Within that marriage, two people are having two completely different *marriages*. One thinks it is great and the other thinks is lousy. Be on one accord; fight for your marriage.

Until you realize that your marriage is important and valuable, until you place value on it, you may wonder what all this Marriage Warfare is about, (1Peter 4:12), *Beloved, think it not strange concerning the fiery trial, which is to try you as though some strange thing happened unto you, but rejoice insomuch as you are partakers of Christ suffering. That when his glory shall be revealed, you may be glad also with exceeding joy.*

Everybody is going through tests and trials. Don't think you're the only one, (1 Peter 5:9). There's always reward for warfare, spoils, in God. After suffering, God will perfect you stablish, strengthen, and settle you, (1 Pe 5:10b), that is, *after* you go through in your marriage, the Lord will perfect, mature, establish, strengthen, and settle your marriage. If you don't understand and appreciate the value of your mate and your marriage when the warfare comes, you may only fight *in* your marriage, instead of fighting for it.

God in His awesome Wisdom will teach your hands to war, (2 Samuel, 22:35, Psalms 18:34, Psalms 144:1). The very thing that you're supposed to have that you're supposed to be ministering to your family and the people you know, and meet is the very same thing that will cause you to have to minister to your mate. Well, it seems so hard. Or that your mate is so-- *whatever.* that could be the Lord teaching your hands to war, honing your gifts and making you produce the Fruit that you're supposed to have.

Rule 106   Have A Good Reward

Have a good reward. Two are better than one and have a good reward for their labor, (Ecc 4:9-11, Col 3:24). Marriage Ed. #106 is more of a gift for your relationship than a **Rule**. Enjoy! It presupposes that you will connect with your mate, *become one,* and do the work with the Lord put you together to do.

Rule 107   Give Due Benevolence

Sex. Give your mate due benevolence, (1 Cor 7:3). Please, your wife, please your husband, do not defraud your mate. Your mate's body is yours and your body is your mate's. Please your marriage partner sexually; it is a gift from God. Do not withhold sex, comfort, touch, eye contact or physical love from your mate, no matter how angry you are. Withholding praise and sex from your spouse for punishment or your own purposes is witchcraft.

Rule 36: *Be Angry But Sin Not,* **Rule 37,** *Do Not Let the Sun Go Down on Your Wrath.* Fight, if you must, with one another, but when the sun goes down--, due benevolence. Please your mate, right around midnight, tender mercies. See **Rule 38.** Are you ready to play fair? Are you ready to do it? As God says? Is your mate? Yes. You're ready for marriage.

Rule 108   Reconcile Your Emotions

Reconcile your emotions, (2 John 2). If everything about your previous failed relationships with your ex was *their* fault, you are not ready to marry or remarry. Come to terms with your own emotions. How do you feel about previous relationships? What part did you have in their demise?

If you're *perfect,* you better start praying for your intended mate now so they can learn to live with you and your perfection. You are not perfect, sorry. Your problem is control. You couldn't control the previous mate, so he/she became imperfect in your eyes. Think on that. Regarding the previous relationship, forgive, drop the bitterness cancel the war in your mind and in the Courts and get on with life. Sharing your present life and your future is the gift you want to give to your new mate, not your past. *You* don't even want your past. Why do you think your new mate would be interested in it?

Rule 109 Finish Your *First* Marriage

Finish your *first* marriage completely, (Hebrews 10:9). Say goodbye. Leave your ex completely physically, emotionally, and spiritually. Cut all soul ties, minister to your children. But finish the divorce. Even though God hates divorce when He separated people in the Bible, one or both either died or was sent to other countries or cities. Take a divorce or separation class if necessary. Some may need a class called Marriage Recovery or Divorce Recovery.

Rule 110 Prosper In Your Soul

Prosper in your Soul, (3 John 2). An important part of soul prosperity is being able to spend time with your spouse as well as away from. How you get along with or without others is a measure of soul prosperity as well. If you don't trust your mate out of your sight, that's a problem for counseling and or deliverance—on yours or their part. Learn to be content and satisfied; that leads to gratitude. God and spouse will appreciate it.

Soul prosperity will help your personal health and finances, as well as the health of your marriage grow Fruit. Every Fruit of the Spirit feeds, nourishes, and prosperous your soul and are needed for your marriage.

Rule 111 Trust Your Mate

Trust your mate. Your soul prosperity is contingent on trusting your mate, actually trusting anyone. It is too much work to follow people around asking 40 questions about their travels and contacts. It is just not worth it. If you can't trust your mate, pray and ask God to help you **trust**. If you can't trust your mate, trust God *for* your mate. Trusting that He has all things in His hand.

Rule 112 Be Consistent

Be consistent, (1 Corinthians 7:37, 15:58). No matter if what is going on is in your favor or not, be consistent in mood and behavior towards your mate.

Rule 113 Be Flexible

Be flexible. Teachability is part of flexibility, (Jeremiah 17:23). Yes, be consistent and flexible. Learn to be what you need to be in truth and honesty with your mate. You must be flexible to grow without breaking. Grow. (See Philippians 4:12.)

Rule 114   Counseling, Yes, or No?

Counseling. Yes, or no? Do not take your spouse to the marriage counselor to be *fixed*. Once again, your perfection raises its ugly head. What audacity to take your mate to have the counselor *fix* him or her. The one doing the taking has **control issues**. Pray.

If you or your mate have no desire to read this book, take the quizzes or discuss your differences in order to reconcile them before marriage. That's a problem. Pay attention if you are not married, not agreeing to, trusting and or submitting to counseling is not a positive thing. Is it ego? Pride, fear, shame. Can't submit? Unteachable? Need deliverance?

If you're already married and aren't interested in making your marriage better or learning more about your mate if one of you needs marriage counseling, **both** of you need it. Don't wait until you're fighting now. Go now to improve your marriage, however, in wise counsel, there is safety, (Proverbs 11:14).

The next three **MARRIAGE ED. Rules** have to deal with social etiquette. The Bible does say let all things be done decently in an order and it means etiquette, (1 Corinthians 14:40). The people of God, those in the church, are not exempt from etiquette and order; they should be modeling it for society.

Rule 115   No Bridal Showers

No showers. Second, marriages and people who have children do not have bridal showers, or wear white in the marriage ceremony. Also, it is not common to have a large church wedding. It is not considered in good taste to have a large church wedding, bride in white symbolizing purity ...of course, do as you choose. But now you know.

Rule 116   No Housewarmings

Second homes do not receive housewarmings. You already have a home, and you already live there. You don't need more stuff. Continuing to beg for gifts by having shower after shower is a poverty mindset and will keep you poor looking for handouts from people. If you just want the fellowship, a classy way to invite people is to write, *No Gifts* on the invitations that clearly states that your motive is to enjoy the company of the guest. Have them see your new home and maybe even bless it but not hit them up for money and household items. t's your house no one made you buy it.

Rule 117   No Baby Showers
No baby showers.

1. Second, children and up do not receive baby showers. Only first babies of usually very young parents.
2. And baby showers are not given by family members for those first babies.
3. Baby showers are not given by the mother to be moms. Do not throw yourself a shower. If you want gifts, you want gifts, but this is not proper etiquette.
4. Baby showers are typically given by friends of the mothers- to-be.
5. It is now acceptable, even fashionable, and expected for men to attend baby showers, especially the baby's father.

The next **MARRIAGE ED., Rules** are based on my books of *The Wilderness Romance (series).* They are not reasons to get married.

Rule 118   Leave Home First

Leave home first, (Genesis 12:1-2, Ruth 2:11). If you haven't grown up and left home yet, it's probably not a good time to get married. Because you want to be out of your parents' house is not a valid reason for matrimony. Just because you want to leave home, does it mean you have to get married? Just move.

Rule 119   Peer Pressure

Peer pressure. If you're not getting married of your own volition and decision, do not because your friend is getting married, is only peer pressure. Don't be a copycat. Don't get married because your friend, relative, or grandma is pressuring you. Do not get married until you know that you know it's time and he or she is the right one. Pray. Ask God listen, receive godly, not soulish counsel. Believe in what you believe in and stand for it. Don't be a hypocrite. (See **Rule 33**.)

Rule 120   Stay In Circulation

Stay in circulation. Jealousy is a work of the flesh. It is first cousins to *competition*. If you are marrying a person to keep someone else from marrying him or her, to get him or her out of circulation while moving in jealousy, competition, selfishness, and pure meanness, you're asking for trouble. You are taking yourself out of circulation as well. Don't do it. Stay in circulation. Even if you know your purpose. The wrong mate could mess up your entire life.

If you are married and did this, repent, apologize to God. Ask Him to redeem the time. Decide to *agape* your mate and ask God to be in your marriage. You'd be surprised what God and your good decision can do. If you feel or know that your spouse married you for this or a similar reason, do the same as above. (See **Rule 34:** *Put Away Envy and Jealousy*).

Rule 121   Marry Your Mate, Not His *Stuff*

Marry, your mate, not his or her *stuff*, (Proverbs 11:28). Marriage is one human being, making a lifelong covenant with another. It is not one person marrying the bank account, wallet, money, or any other material goods of another. Humans cannot marry *things*, even if those things are *attached* to the other human. It won't work. Don't do it. Money can't buy you love, and money can't be your love. Those who marry for money because they like his or her material stuff will be tested in that. What if a reversal of fortune comes? What if the person never was rich but only seemed, appeared, or acted well off? Do not be deceived. Do not trust in riches but seek first the Kingdom and all other things will be added unto you, (Luke 12:31, 1Timothy 6:17).

Rule 122   Pull Your Weight

If you're not prepared to pull your weight in a marriage, don't marry. If you plan to marry to be taken care of if you're lazy, especially if you are a man --forget about it. Your harebrained scheme will not work. Eventually you will find failure and possibly misery staring you in the face. Do not get married for green card, ATM card, or credit card. If you are such a person, repent, become productive. You don't work, you don't eat, (1 Thessalonians 3:10).

Emotionally, be a lively stone. The marriage cannot be built with deadweight, (1 Peter 2:4-5). No one is interested in having to cheer you up and make you laugh every day, all day.

Pull your weight, spiritually. Do you pray? Enter into spiritual warfare? Is every problem in the marriage yours? Every financial problem, every emotional problem, and every spiritual problem are they are they problems you can avoid but you don't? Are you even trying? Are you praying?

Rule 123   Status, Prestige

Status and prestige and the title are three things that come with many marriages. Marry, because of love, purpose and to spend your life with your mate instead of what he or she can offer you. You can go to Vital Statistics in your city and change your name to anything you want it to be. You don't have to get married for a *title*. Go to school. Earn a degree. *Become* who you're supposed to be, instead of marrying to be in the *shadow* of what/who someone else already is. Worse, if you're planning to be in the shadow of what someone else *will be* or *hopes to be* with no dreams of your own—, where's the Purpose God put in you?

If you sell yourself to someone, they **own** you, plain and simple. That's called slavery or prostitution. Marrying in exchange for *tangible stuff* or *titles* is **selling yourself**.

Men have been guilty of marrying and to advance careers to give appearance of being a family man, if that's what you married her for, what's in it for her?

Rule 124   Biological Clock

Tick tock. The biological clock is not a valid reason to marry just anyone. Assuming the biological clock actually exists, it may be a valid reason to get married. Children need a mother and a father, and a wise man will know the times in which he is living. You would not have a Sweet 16 party when you get 65. There is a time for everything, and everything is beautiful in its time, (Ecclesiastes 3:11). Have a family, so your name will not be cut off from the Earth.

Abraham and his wife were about 100 years old when they had Isaac. God's running the clock of destiny. Ask Him if you are operating on the destiny clock or some other.

Rule 125   No Sex

No sex. There are flesh marriages, but there are not many wise men after the flesh. Not many mighty, not many noble, (1 Corinthians 1:26). This book is written to help you avoid getting into or living in a flesh marriage. Too many through the ages have gotten married while in lust, thinking it was love. That's one reason why sex should never come before marriage. It's so you will know the difference. Sex is not the reason enough to marry.

If you are married and got married for sex, I hope the sex is good, but have you evolved into *relationship* with your mate? Can you? Get to know the rest of your mate, not just his or her body. Love waits. Lust doesn't. Love endures. Lust can't. Love, encourages, builds up. Lust coerces and destroys.

Rule 126   Just For Fun?
Just for fun, just to say you did it. No! Marriage is not an experiment or something you add to your resume.

Rule 127   Not Just An Event
Do not get married for the event, the dress, the reception, or the pictures. Marriage is not just an event. It has discipline and a lifestyle. Just as prayer is not an event, but a discipline. In our lifestyle, the Disciplines of Marriage can help your prayer life and your prayer life can help your marriage. Events entertain and distract. Discipline pleases God, while it edifies and grows you up.

Rule 128   Remedy for Sin?

For ages, people have tried **to remedy sin**. Adam and Eve hid in the trees after they sinned. Duh! The same place they sinned --in the trees, sin makes people as dumb as the dirt of which they are made.

A pregnancy! Marriage won't cover that up. The *seed* was already sown in *whoredoms*. If you get married to make sure that all become a family unit and all parties, get what they need to exist in this unit, that's a different story. If you marry to avoid shame, you can't--, because the shame is automatically sown in there. If you married to punish yourself for having illegal sex, you'll pretty much be successful at that.

If you cannot *contain* yourself, marry, else, *contain* yourself. Keep your pants on. If you're not married, sex isn't for you. You know the toaster, blender and all that stuff that couples get as wedding gifts? They also get **sex** as a gift from God. Sex is a gift that you do not get legally until you get married. Sex is not for single people. Marriage can't remedy sin. If so, Jesus could just marry the church before, or outside of salvation, deliverance, and justification. Salvation remedies sin, marriage to the Lamb comes *after* salvation.

Marriage in the Earth should come *after* salvation, after you are saved.

Rule 129   Find Favor

Be willing to **find favor in and discover favorable things about your mate** Favor is good regard, approval or support. It is the cause of special treatment, partiality, privilege, often caused by affection. We all want the favor of God and in marriage one should also have the favor of his or her spouse.

Note the favorable things about your mate and dwell on those things. Speak on those things. Think on those things. Are you willing to look for what's right about your mate rather than what's wrong? If not, don't marry.

If you're already married and or criticizing and critical, you need to just ask Jesus to change your negative ways so you will be enjoyable to be around.

Endeavor to find favor in your mate's eyes, (Proverbs 3:34). Solomon expounds that the way to find favor in the eyes of God and man is to move in Truth and Mercy. Those two things should not be foreign to any marriage partner. We've spoken in **Rule 47:** *Kindness* and in **Rule 18:** *Grace,* as well as

Speaking the Truth in Love, **Rule 20** about other things that are important for a successful marriage. There's a reliability that comes with the balance of those three things and that is attractive to any person. Add, *Obeying God,* **Rule 59** of **MARRIAGE ED**. As we continue in Proverbs, we learn that these Rules have promise-- finding favor is the promise. When you give Mercy and stay in Truth. (Finding favor, see Ruth 2:13, 1 Samuel 25:8, and 2 Samuel, 15:25.)

Rule 130   The One Another Disciplines

The One Another Disciplines are for marriage too. Especially:

Love one another, even as I have loved you. (John 13:34, 1 Thessalonians 4:19, 1 John 3:11, 1 John 3:23, 1John 4:4-7, 11-12 2 John 1:5).

Prefer one another, (Romans 12:10).

Admonish one another, (Romans 15:14, Colossians 3:16). If one of you is about to make a huge mistake, the other must admonish him, or her, telling the truth in love, (Ephesians 4:15). Admonishment leads to correction. (See Rule 20.)

Salute one another with a holy kiss, (Roman 16:16, 2 Corinthians 13:12) *Smooches gracias.* Your mate will be grateful for kisses.

Serve one another, (Galatians 5:13).

Forbear one another in love, (Ephesians 4:2, Col 3:16. **Rule 17.**)

Forgive one another. (Ephesians 4:32, 2 Corinthians 5:18. See **Rule 49.**)

Teach one another. (Colossians 3:16. See **Rules 69** and **99.**)

Comfort one another (1Thessalonians 4:18. See **Rules 107** and **131**)

Edify one another, (1 Thessalonians 5:11, Jude 1:20, **Rule 18**).

Pray for one another, (Ephesians 1:16, **Rules 94, 95, 98**).

Pray with one another. (See **Rule 92.**)

Worship The Lord with one another. (See **Rule 64.**)

Help one another. If one falls, (Ecclesiastes 4:10). Minister, reconciliation to one another, not condemnation, (2 Corinthians 5:18). The message, if God is not holding anything against you, I'm not either.

Restore one another in love, (Galatians 6:1).

Share with one another having all things in common, (Acts 2:44).

Look one another in the face, (2 Kings 14:8).

Do not deny your countenance to your mate. There is love, health, and healing in it. When God looks on His people. He blesses them. When He expresses displeasure, He turns his face away from them. Your mate feels rejection when you withhold your face. If that's what you desire, reread the **Malice, (Meanness) Rule, #31**. In ancient cultures, the sick were not to be looked upon. John and Peter changed that when they said, *"Look on us,"* to the man to whom they ministered healing, (Acts 3:4-7)

Touch one another. There's healing in the touch and by the laying on of hands. This is why personal massages are therapeutic, (1 Timothy 4:14, Hebrews 6:2. See **Rule 107**.)

Do not hate one another. *Do not let the sun go down on your wrath,* (Ephesians 4:26). Love is a choice. Love is life. Choose life. Choose to love.

Do not condemn one another or devour one another (Romans 1.).

Do not trick one another. Do not lie or steal from one another. Let no man deceive you, (Matthew 2:4, 1 Corinthians 3:18, Ephesians 5:6, 2 Thessalonians 2:3m 1John 3:7).

Do not use one another deal honestly with one another.

Whatever good things you do to your mate will be done again, and to you, (Ephesians 6:8) and, *whatever bad thing,* (Galatians 6:7-8).

Rule 131   Take Care of One Another

Take care of one another, whether or not you say that *in sickness or in health* thing, you must **take care of one another**. No one will take care of you better than your spouse. And don't say your mother because you should have left mom by **Rule 27**, when you begin your cleaving process, when you begin the process of *becoming*. My husband or wife? Here, both spouses need to use **Rule 66** and remain teachable. One of you will help the other eat better, drink more water and another of you, or the same someone will take the other out for walks, swimming, or all out body training. Love yourselves TOGETHER.

Rule 132   Exercise

Exercise. Take care of yourself. Exercise together. Here I am changing an often-quoted passage, *Bodily exercise profits if you want to stay little,* (1Timothy 4:8). A healthy, fit body is very attractive to the opposite sex. Your marriage partner is <u>the</u> opposite sex after marriage, there's only one opposite sex or marriage partner. Stay healthy and sexy.

Further, exercising together builds intimacy. Don't just exercise with your friends. Move your body with your husband or wife.

Stay attractive for yourself and your mate. Do not only get gussied up to go to the office or church, fix up, look, and smell nice for your spouse at home.

Rule 133   Stay Healthy

Stay healthy. Don't burden the person you say your love with avoidable trips to the doctor, medical and pharmacy expenses, diseases, illnesses, and untimely death. Do not renege on your promise to grow old together. Keep your word. Stay healthy. Stay alive.

A diet is an event. Eating well is a lifestyle.

What does my exercise routine look like now per week?

_____

What does my mates weekly exercise routine look like?

_____

How do they compare and contrast?

_____

Do we have any sports in common?

_____

It would be best to have at least one sport or exercise related activity and comment. I challenge you to find one.

What needs to be changed?

_____

Are you willing to make these changes?

_____

Answer the same questions above regarding you and your mate's eating habits.

Rule 134   For Spiritual Purpose

Get married for spiritual purpose. What is your purpose for being on Earth and in the Kingdom of God? Don't know. Then you're really not ready to be married. Why? Because until you know, you don't know if your purpose involves your being married or not, or who it involves your being married to. One wrong step could mess up a whole lot of good. If you're not supposed to be married to him or her, he or she is not supposed to be married to you either. And you've each interfered with the other's purpose for being here and messed up his or her life. Think about it. Find your purpose first. Begin to walk in it. Find out from God if you're supposed to be married to him or her, or to whom. Find out what your personal, individual mission is. Then you'll know how to submit to it.

It would be ever so wise to know the mission of the person that you're marrying as well, so you can also submit to it, Huh? I thought only women submitted to missions. Not so, they both submit to one another as unto the Lord, (Ephesians

5:20). You submit to each other's **mission** as well as to the *mission* of the marriage. **See Marriage Ed., Rule 68**.

Rule 135   Because God Said So

Get married because God said so. (See **Marriage Ed., Rule 99.**) God began marrying folks as soon as He made them. Of course, He made full-fledged adults, then. He gave Wisdom, jobs, and purpose. God also said, **"Be fruitful and multiply."** It is considered spiritually illegal to have children without first being married. Get married and be fruitful and multiply. Subdue the earth and the works of the enemy. Sit in dominion because God said to do it. Obedience is better than to sacrifice. (See **Rule 124**.)

Rule 136   For Righteous Seed

Get married for righteous seeds, (Malachi 2:15). God is ever looking for righteous seeds. Isaac was a righteous seed, as was Jesus. Ishmael was not because the two were not in the marriage covenant. Ishmael was a flesh child. When two become married, as the Lord instructs, He then has an instrument to bring righteous children to the Earth. Baptist John was a righteous seed. Samuel.

164

Samson. God instructed their parents exactly how to bring up their children before they were ever born. God is looking for more of that, instead of always having to fix things after a mess up.

I've never seen the righteous forsaken or their seed beg bread, (Psalm 37:25). Many are the afflictions of the Righteous, but the Lord delivers him out of them all (Psalms 34:19). And did he not make one that he might seek a godly seed? (Malachi 2:15).

Rule 137   Meet the Children

Meet the children. In today's world of second and third marriages, make sure you meet the children no matter how old are young they are, whether they will be living with you or not. As said, the fruit doesn't fall far from the tree. Are the children like your mate, or exact opposites?

How is your mate with his or her children? A good parent, pushover? A mean old hag? An insensitive jerk? Look into that now.

Rule 138 Meet the Exes

Meet the Exes-- if they're still around. It's really a shame that this needs to be a rule for marriage. But in these days.... How does your intended relate to his or her ex? Good, bad, ugly? What is their dynamic? Can you stand it? Can you deal with it? Do you think it'll change anytime soon? Ever? Whether or not you can help them is not the answer, unless you are a Counselor. Eyes wide open.

Rule 139 To Establish Covenant

Get married to establish covenant with your mate. Get married. You become *one* as a forerunner to Jesus marrying the Church. Get married so young people can see how it's done. Be a role model to them. Be a role model in the Earth.

Rule 140 For Spiritual Warfare

Get married for warfare. Form a power tool that will put up to 10,000 to flight. Become a weapon against the devil. It is expected that you will pray together and even enter into spiritual warfare together. How do I know? Because stuff will come at you that will cause you to have to do warfare together. You get engaged to be married sooner or later, but especially after marriage you will engage the enemy. With God be victorious.

Never engage your spouse in warfare. Swords and words are sharp and dangerous, (Hebrews 4:12).

Get married because you want to be greater than you are as a single; get married because you will put 1000 to Flight, two, 10,000 (Deuteronomy 32:30).

Do it to help others do it for the glory that God will get. See **Rule 105**, *Fight For Your Marriage* and

Rule 141 To Glorify God

Get married to glorify God. If you're ready to glorify God in your marriage, you're ready to get married. The Good Book says that he who is married is looking more to please his wife than God, but that she who is married is concerned with pleasing her husband. This is true of flesh marriages, but when two get married with spiritual purpose, because God says so, and walk in the Spirit as much as possible, they will be pleasing to God, just because of their union. And in their union, they will seek to please God. Even if the couple can't see any further than next year and they want to *have a boy* or two years from now when they want to *have a girl* and then get their first home together, God can see clearly what he wants out of the marriage. If God allowed the marriage, He will work it together for good. What good? Don't know. All of it may not be obvious this week, this year, even in your lifetime.

God could be teaching your hands to war. He could be binding two together for ministry. You two could be parents of righteous seed or their great grandparents. God's ways are higher than ours. That's why you have to trust Him. He can't tell you every detail of everything. Most of it is on a need-to-know basis and you wouldn't understand all of what you were told if He told you anyway.

Glory to God!

If you have no intentions of glorifying Him, being served, taken care of, and having your flesh needs met, don't get married.

Why were you created? Why are you here on Earth?

Not knowing this before marriage could be an adventure to you and your spouse, or it could traumatize you both. It's best to know as soon as possible.

Why was your mate created? _____-

_____

Does your mate know the above?

_____

Does your mate know why you were created?

_____

What is your purpose?

_____

What is your mate's purpose?

_____

What are you and your mate's *joint* purposes in the Earth?

How will you or the two of you, together glorify God?

_____

_____

Rule 142   Be Faithful

Be faithful (Proverbs 2:6, 1 Corinthians 4:2, 1Timothy 3:11, Revelations 2:10). *Whatever you do, do it with your whole heart, soul, and body* (Mark 12:30). Be disciplined. Be faithful. Bring joy and success to your mate and your marriage. Bring glory to God.

Rule 143   Respect Other Marriages

Respect other marriages, whether married or not, respect your own marriage as well as others, because you will reap what you sow (Galatians 6:7). Showing disrespect will cause you to reap disrespect.

Rule 144   Be Creative

Be creative, find new ways to love and appreciate, and learn new things about your mate, who is God's creation. Bring new activities to your marriage. Take a cooking class, bungee jump, do something new. Always.

Rule 145   Expect the Best

Expect the best from your mate in your marriage. Always be expecting.

Rule 146   Surprise Your Mate

Surprise your mate, if he or she likes surprises, show that you care enough to find him or her special gifts.

Rule 147   Study Together

Study together. Study both your Bible and read other books together. Stay teachable. Stay interesting. Learn new things. Learn new things together.

Rule 148   Get Away

Get away together regularly. Don't wear yourself out by forgetting to go on vacation together. Sometimes you may include other couples, your children, or relatives. There should be at least one special trip a year for just the two of you.

Rule 149   Have Dates

Have dates. Get a room. Even when you can't leave town, send the kids to Grandma's, or get a babysitter, book a hotel room, do something exciting and interesting with your mate. You should have no fewer than two dates a month with your spouse. Every week would be great.

Rule 150   Live!

Live. Marriage takes your salvation to the next level. What you know you do in your intimate marital relationship. Trials come. Tests come. But, together, you get through it. Marriage is the ultimate One-Another and *agape* love test. If you can't *agape* your covenant partner, who can you *agape?*

If you can't *agape* God with whom you are in covenant. Who can you *agape?* Again, I say that marriage to the Lamb is our destiny and goal. Our Earth marriages are on the job training for that Eternal Union.

Jesus brought us Salvation so we can live. Salvation brings life. Jesus came that you may have life and have it more abundantly, (John 10:10). Be married, enjoy and live. *Love life and see good days,* (1 Peter 3:10a).

Be successful in your Earth marriage. Marriage to the Lamb is our ultimate goal, so be outstanding in your Earth marriage so that God sees that you are *Marriage Material.*

Dear Reader

Thank you for acquiring and reading this book. I pray for that you have a long, lovely, and victorious marriage that glories God and brings you joy, peace, abundance and beautiful, righteous seed.

May all the blessings of His Name be yours.

Amen.

Dr. Marlene Miles

Dr. Marlene Miles has served in Ministry for 20+ years. She holds two doctorate degrees in Ministry and is a dentist by day. Her joy is to share what God gives her.

Enjoy her messages on the Dr. Miles Youtube Channel.

Christian books by this author

AK: Adventures of the Agape Kid

AMONG SOME THIEVES

As My Soul Prospers

Behave

Churchzilla (The Wanna-Be Bride of Christ)

The Coco-So-So Correct Show

Demons Hate Questions

The Throne of Grace, *Courtroom Prayers*

Triangular Powers (4-Book Series)

> Powers Above: Triagular Powers
>
> SUNBLOCK: Triangular Powers
>
> Do Not Swear by the Moon: *Triangular Powers*
>
> Starstruck: Triangular Powers

Warfare Prayer Against Poverty

When the Devourer is Rebuked

The Wilderness Romance (Series)

> The Social Wilderness
>
> The Sexual Wilderness
>
> The Spiritual Wilderness

Other Journals & Devotionals by this author:

The Cool of the Day – Journal times spent with God

got HEALING? Verses for Life

got HOPE? Verses for Life

got LOVE? Verses for Life

He Hears Us, Prayer Journal *in 4 different colors*

I Have A Star, Dream Journal *in styles for kids, teen,* I Have A Star, Guided Prayer Journal, *2 styles: Boy or Girl*

J'ai une Etoile, Journal des Reves

Let Her Dream, Dream Journal *multiple colors*

Men Shall Dream, Dream Journal, *(blue or black)*

My Favorite Prayers (in 4 styles)

My Sowing Journal (in three different colors)

Tengo una Estrella, Diario de Sueños

Illustrated children's books by this author:

Big Dog (8-book series)

Do Not Say That to Me

Every Apple

Fluff the Clouds

I Love You All Over the World

Imma Dance

The Jump Rope

Kiss the Sun

The Masked Man

Not During a Pandemic

Push the Wind

What If?

Wiggle, Wiggle; Giggle, Giggle

Worry About Yourself

You Did Not Say Goodbye to Me

ALPHABETICAL INDEX

SUBJECT INDEX
OF **MARRIAGE ED.** RULES

Be Angry, Sin Not, Rule 36

Be Debt Free, Rule 101

Do Not Be Drunk, Rule 65

Get Rid of the Pornography, Rule 56

Let Not the Sun Go Down on Your Wrath, Rule 17

Peace & Joy, Rule 100

Put Away Filthiness, Rule 57

Prosper in Your Soul, Rule 110

<u>Discipline</u>

Be Angry, Sin Not, Rule 36

Bear Fruit, Rule 17

Do Not Be Drunk, Rule 65

Don't Hang Out with the Disobedient, rule 64

Exercise: Take are of Yourself, Rule 132

Follow God, Rule 51

Forgive One Another, Rule 49

Fornication & *Whoremongering*, Rule 54

Lay Aside Malice, Rule 31

Let Not the Sun Go Down on Your Wrath, Rule 37

Marriage Has Disciplines, Rule 3

New commandment, Rule 14

Obey God, Rule 62

One-Another Disciplines, Rule 130

Put Away Covetousness & Idolatry, Rule 58

Walk in *Agape* Love, Rule 52

Disciplines of Marriage
Marriage Has Disciplines, Rule 3

Divorce
Finish Your First Marriage

Dominion
For Warfare, Rule 140

Have Abundance, Rule 42

God Says So, Rule 135

Pray Always, Rule 94

Use Grace, Give Grace, Rule 18

Edification
Boldness & Teaching, Rule 99

No corrupt Communication, Rule 44

Remain Teachable, Rule 69

Use Grace, Give Grace, Rule 18

Etiquette
No Baby Shower, Rule 117

No Bridal Shower, Rule 115

No Housewarming, Rule 116

Evil

Put Away Guile, Rule 32

Put Away Evil Talk, Rule 35

Refrain From Evil & Guile, Rule 102

Shalt-Not VI, Rule 9

Family/Children

Be Debt Free, Rule 101

Children, Obey Father & Mother, Rule 85

Glorify God, Rule 141

No Unequal Yokes, Rule 104

Righteous Seeds, Rule 136

Shalt-Not V, Rule 8

Tick Tock, Biological Clock, Rule 124

Favor

Find Favor, Love, Rule 129

Flesh, *Works of the*

Fornication & *Whoremongering*, Rule 54

Lay Aside Malice, Rule 31

Let Not the Sun Go Down on Your Wrath, Rule 37

Put Away Covetousness & Idolatry, Rule 58

Put Away Envy & Jealousy, Rule 34

Put Away Evil Talk, Rule 35

Put Away Filthiness, Rule 57

Put Away Foolish Talking & Jesting, Rule 59

Put Away Guile, Rule 32

Put Away Hypocrisy, Rule 33

Put Away Uncleanness, Rule 55

Put Off Lying, Rule 30

Put Off the Old Man, Rule 28

Put That Away, Rule 46

Refrain From Evil & Guile, Rule 102

Friends

Meet the Church Members, Rule 84

Meet the Co-Workers, Rule 83

Meet the Friends, Rule 82

Peer Pressure, Rule 119

Don't Hang Out with the Disobedient, Rule 64

Fruit of the Spirit

Be Faithful, Rule 142

Be Kind to One Another, Rule 47

Be Tenderhearted, Rule 48

Fight For Your Marriage, Rule 105

Fruit, *in general:*

Peace & joy, Rule 100

Suffer Well, Rule 103

Giving

Give No Place to the Devil, Rule 39

Husband, Give For Wife, Rule 73

Share, Rule 43

Sex!!! Give Due Benevolence, Rule 107

Use Grace, Give Grace, Rule 18

God's Glory

Be Fruitful, Rule 142

For Warfare, Rule 140

Glorify God, Rule 141

Grace & Mercy

Use Grace, Give Grace, Rule 18

Tender Mercies, Rule 38

Guarding Yourself & Marriage

Give No Place to the Devil, Rule 39

Fornication & *Whoremongering*, Rule 54

Sex!!! Give Due Benevolence, Rule 107

Remain Teachable, Rule 69

Also, see all of Spiritual Warfare

Trust Your Mate, Rule 111

www.ingramcontent.com/pod-product-compliance
Lightning Source LLC
LaVergne TN
LVHW051403080426
835508LV00022B/2957